The $100M Sales Playbook

The Secret to Turning Leads into Loyal Customers

Iftekhar Uddin Rizvi

Table of Contents

Chapter 17   129

5 Best Salespeople of This World and Their Success Secrets

Chapter 18   138

Action Plan and Next Steps

Acknowledgements

I would like to express my heartfelt gratitude to everyone who contributed to the creation of The $100M Sales Playbook. Thank you to my dedicated team of researchers and editors for their unwavering support and commitment. Special thanks to my mentors and advisors for their valuable guidance. I am also indebted to the readers who have embraced this book and allowed it to make a positive impact. Your encouragement and feedback have been invaluable.

Introduction

Welcome to a journey that will transform your sales approach. "The $100M Sales Playbook: The Secret to Turning Leads into Loyal Customers" is not just another sales book; it's your secret weapon for conquering the diverse world of human nature.

In this captivating guide, we'll explore the complex tapestry of the American consumer landscape, a dynamic canvas painted with various personalities, preferences, and purchasing behaviors. Understanding human nature is key to unlocking unprecedented success in sales. Technology is evolving, but human connection remains at the heart of every successful transaction.

The modern sales professional knows that true mastery lies in adapting and connecting with different customer personalities. You're not just selling a product; you're creating an experience tailored to each customer's unique preferences and motivations.

Imagine effortlessly resonating with your customers, building rapport seamlessly, and anticipating their needs before they even express them. The benefits are transformative: increased sales, enhanced customer loyalty, and a reputation as a sales virtuoso.

In the chapters that follow, we'll dive into the intricacies of various customer archetypes, decoding their motivations, preferences, and communication styles. Whether you're engaging with trend-setting Trailblazers, analytical Thinkers, or socially conscious Advocates, this guide equips you with the tools to tailor your approach effectively.

Prepare for a sales journey where each interaction is a masterpiece, a symphony composed to resonate with the distinct chords of individual personalities. Let "The $100M Sales Playbook: The Secret to Turning Leads into Loyal Customers " be your companion in mastering the art of selling, connecting, and influencing – a journey that will not only elevate your sales game but also redefine what it means to be a true sales professional. Get ready to unleash the power of personalization and sell like the pro you were meant to be!

Chapter 1

The Psychology of Selling

In the competitive world of sales, understanding human psychology is a crucial factor in achieving success. Salespeople who possess a deep understanding of the psychological principles that influence customer behavior are better equipped to build rapport, identify customer needs, and ultimately close deals.

Importance of Understanding Human Psychology in Sales

Understanding the human psychology is essential for salespeople for several reasons:

- **Building Rapport:** By understanding the customer's psychological makeup, salespeople can tailor their approach to establish a connection and build rapport. This rapport-building process is crucial for creating a positive atmosphere and fostering trust, which are essential for successful sales interactions.

- **Identifying Customer Needs:** Customers often have unspoken needs and desires that may not be immediately apparent. Salespeople who are skilled in reading body language, listening actively, and asking probing questions can uncover these hidden needs and tailor their sales pitch accordingly.

- **Overcoming Objections:** Objections are a natural part of the sales process, and salespeople must be prepared to handle them effectively. By understanding the psychological factors that drive objections, such as fear of change or perceived risk, salespeople can develop strategies to address these concerns and move the sales process forward.

- **Closing the Deal:** The final step in the sales process is closing the deal. Salespeople who understand the psychology of persuasion can employ techniques such as social proof, scarcity, and reciprocity to increase the likelihood of a positive outcome.

Basic Principles of Human Psychology

- **Perception:** Perception refers to how individuals receive and interpret information from their surroundings. Salespeople should be aware of how customers perceive their products or services, as well as the factors that influence these perceptions, such as personal experiences, cultural background, and social norms.

- **Motivation:** Motivation is the driving force behind human behavior. Salespeople need to understand what motivates customers to make purchasing decisions. Common motivators include the desire for pleasure, avoidance of pain, social recognition, and self-actualization.

- **Emotion:** Emotions play a significant role in the buying process. Positive emotions, such as excitement or joy, can increase a customer's likelihood of making a purchase, while negative emotions, such as fear or anxiety, can have the opposite effect. Salespeople should strive to create a positive emotional experience for customers throughout the sales interaction.

- **Cognition:** Cognition refers to the mental processes involved in acquiring, storing, and processing information. Salespeople should be aware of how customers process and retain information, as well as the factors that influence these processes, such as attention, memory, and decision-making.

Psychological Biases and Their Impact on Buying Behavior

Customers are often influenced by psychological biases, which are systematic errors in thinking that can lead to irrational decision-making. Salespeople can leverage these biases to increase sales by understanding how they work and using them to their advantage.

Common Cognitive Biases that Affect Customer Decision-Making:

- **Confirmation Bias:** Customers tend to seek out information that confirms their existing beliefs and disregard information that contradicts them. Salespeople can use this bias by providing information that supports the customer's initial interest in the product or service.

- **Framing Effect:** The way information is presented can influence customer preferences. Salespeople can use this bias by framing their sales pitch in a way that highlights the benefits of their product or service.

- **Reciprocity:** Customers feel obligated to return favors. Salespeople can use this bias by providing small favors, such as free samples or discounts, to increase the likelihood of a purchase.

- **Social Proof:** Customers are more likely to purchase a product or service if they see that others have done so. Salespeople can use this bias by highlighting customer testimonials, reviews, or social media endorsements.

How to Leverage Psychological Biases to Increase Sales:

- **Use Positive Framing:** Frame your sales pitch in a way that emphasizes the benefits and positive aspects of your product or service.

- **Offer Reciprocity:** Provide small favors or incentives to increase the likelihood of a purchase.

- **Highlight Social Proof:** Share customer testimonials, reviews, or social media endorsements to demonstrate the popularity of your product or service.

- **Avoid Loss Aversion:** Emphasize the potential losses or negative consequences of not purchasing your product or service.

Ethical Considerations When Using Psychological Principles in Sales:

While understanding and leveraging psychological principles can be an effective sales strategy, it is important to do so ethically. Salespeople should avoid using deceptive or manipulative tactics that exploit customer vulnerabilities. Instead, they should focus on providing accurate information, building trust, and helping customers make informed decisions.

Understanding Customer Needs and Wants

Customers have different types of needs that influence their purchasing decisions:

- **Functional Needs:** These are practical needs that relate to the specific features and benefits of a product or service.

- **Emotional Needs:** These are needs that relate to how a product or service makes the customer feel.

- **Social Needs:** These are needs that relate to how a product or service helps the customer fit in with their social group.

How to Identify and Understand Customer Needs Through Active Listening and Questioning:

- **Active Listening:** Pay attention to what the customer is saying, both verbally and nonverbally. Ask clarifying questions to ensure understanding.

- **Open-Ended Questions:** Ask questions that cannot be answered with a simple yes or no. This encourages customers to provide more detailed information.

- **Probe for Underlying Needs:** Ask questions to uncover the customer's deeper motivations and desires.

Creating Customer Profiles to Better Understand and Target Different Customer Types:

Customer profiles are detailed descriptions of different customer types, based on their needs, demographics, and buying behavior. Salespeople can use customer profiles to

- **Personalize Sales Pitches:** Tailor their sales pitch to the specific needs and interests of each customer.

- **Target Marketing Efforts:** Identify and target specific customer segments with marketing campaigns.

- **Improve Customer Service:** Understand and meet the needs of different customer types more effectively.

Building Trust and Rapport

Trust is a critical factor in the sales process. Customers are more likely to buy from salespeople they trust and feel a connection with.

The Importance of Trust in the Sales Process:

- **Increased Sales:** Customers who trust a salesperson are more likely to make a purchase.

- **Stronger Relationships:** Trust leads to stronger relationships between salespeople and customers, which can result in repeat business and referrals.

- **Improved Communication:** When there is trust, customers are more likely to be open and honest with salespeople, which leads to better communication and understanding.

Strategies for Building Trust and Rapport with Customers:

- **Be Honest and Transparent:** Honesty is the foundation of trust. Salespeople should be transparent about their products or services and avoid making promises they can't keep.

- **Listen Actively:** Show customers that you are genuinely interested in what they have to say. Active listening demonstrates that you respect their opinions and value their input.

- **Empathize with Customers:** Put yourself in the customer's shoes and try to understand their needs and concerns. Empathy shows that you care about the customer as a person, not just as a potential sale.

- **Be Patient:** Building trust takes time. Don't try to rush the process. Be patient and persistent, and eventually, you will earn the customer's trust.

How to Create a Positive and Professional First Impression:

- **Dress Professionally:** First impressions matter, so dress in a way that is appropriate for your industry and the customer you are meeting.

- **Be Punctual:** Punctuality shows that you respect the customer's time. Aim to arrive at meetings or appointments a few minutes early.

- **Smile and Make Eye Contact:** A smile and direct eye contact convey warmth and confidence.

- **Introduce Yourself Properly:** Introduce yourself clearly and confidently, stating your name, company, and title.

Persuasion and Influence

Persuasion is the process of influencing someone's beliefs, attitudes, or behavior. In sales, persuasion is used to convince customers to buy a product or service.

Basic Principles of Persuasion and Their Relevance to Sales:

- **Reciprocity:** People are more likely to do something for you if you have done something for them. Salespeople can use this principle by offering customers something of value, such as a free sample or discount, in exchange for their purchase.

- **Social Proof:** People are more likely to do something if they see others doing it. Salespeople can use this principle by highlighting customer testimonials, reviews, or social media endorsements.

- **Authority:** People are more likely to be persuaded by someone they perceive as an expert. Salespeople can use this principle by establishing themselves as knowledgeable and trustworthy sources of information.

- **Liking:** People are more likely to be persuaded by someone they like. Salespeople can use this principle by building rapport with customers and creating a positive relationship.

Different Persuasion Techniques and When to Use Them:

- **Direct Persuasion:** This technique involves making a direct request for the sale. It is most effective when the customer is already interested in the product or service and has a low level of resistance.

- **Indirect Persuasion:** This technique involves using more subtle methods to influence the customer's decision, such as providing information, building rapport, or overcoming objections. It is most effective when the customer is not yet ready to buy or has a high level of resistance.

- **Emotional Persuasion:** This technique involves appealing to the customer's emotions to influence their decision. It is most effective when the product or service is associated with strong emotions, such as happiness, fear, or desire.

How to Overcome Customer Objections and Resistance:

- **Listen Actively:** Before responding to an objection, take the time to listen to the customer's concerns and understand their point of view.

- **Acknowledge the Objection:** Let the customer know that you understand their concern and that you are taking it seriously.

- **Address the Objection:** Provide a clear and concise response to the objection. Be sure to focus on the benefits of your product or service and how it can meet the customer's needs.

- **Move Forward:** Once you have addressed the objection, move the conversation forward by asking for the sale or scheduling a follow-up meeting.

Examples and Case Studies

Example 1:

A car salesperson used the principle of reciprocity to increase sales by offering customers a free car wash with every purchase. This small gesture of goodwill made customers more likely to buy from the salesperson, as they felt obligated to return the favor.

Example 2:

A clothing retailer used the principle of social proof to increase sales by displaying customer testimonials and reviews on their website. Seeing that others had positive experiences with the store and its products made customers more likely to make a purchase.

Case Study 1:

Apple is a company that has achieved sales success through understanding human psychology. Apple's products are designed to be user-friendly and aesthetically pleasing, which appeals to customers' emotional needs. The company also uses celebrity endorsements and social media marketing to create a sense of exclusivity and desirability around its products.

Case Study 2:

Starbucks is another company that has achieved sales success through understanding human psychology. Starbucks' stores are designed to be comfortable and inviting, which creates a positive emotional experience for customers. The company also offers a variety of products to appeal to different customer needs, such as coffee, tea, pastries, and sandwiches.

Conclusion

Salespeople can increase their sales by understanding and applying psychological principles in their interactions with customers. By building trust and rapport, using persuasion techniques, and overcoming objections, salespeople can create a positive sales experience that leads to increased sales and customer loyalty.

Actionable Tips for Salespeople

1. Be honest and transparent with customers.

2. Listen actively to customers and empathize with their needs.

3. Create a positive and professional first impression.

4. Use reciprocity to offer customers something of value in exchange for their purchase.

5. Highlight customer testimonials and reviews to demonstrate social proof.

6. Position yourself as an expert in your field to establish authority.

7. Build rapport with customers by finding common ground and showing genuine interest in them.

8. Use direct persuasion when the customer is already interested in the product or service and has a low level of resistance.

9. Use indirect persuasion when the customer is not yet ready to buy or has a high level of resistance.

10. Use emotional persuasion to appeal to the customer's emotions and create a strong desire for the product or service.

Chapter 2

Understanding Customer Needs and Wants

Understanding customer needs and wants is essential for sales success. By understanding what motivates customers to buy, salespeople can tailor their sales approach to meet those needs and increase their chances of closing a sale.

Importance of Understanding Customer Needs and Wants in Sales

- **Increased Sales:** Salespeople who understand customer needs are better able to identify and recommend products or services that meet those needs, leading to increased sales.

- **Improved Customer Satisfaction:** When customers feel that their needs are being met, they are more likely to be satisfied with their purchase and become repeat customers.

- **Stronger Relationships:** Salespeople who take the time to understand their customers' needs build stronger relationships with them, which can lead to increased loyalty and referrals.

- **Competitive Advantage:** In a competitive market, salespeople who understand customer needs have a competitive advantage over those who do not. By meeting customer needs in a way that competitors cannot, salespeople can differentiate themselves and win more business.

How Understanding Customer Needs Can Help Tailor Sales Approach

- **Identify Customer Pain Points:** By understanding customer needs, salespeople can identify the pain points that customers are experiencing. This allows salespeople to position their products or services as solutions to those pain points.

- **Create Value Propositions:** A value proposition is a statement that summarizes the benefits of a product or service and how it meets customer needs. Salespeople who understand customer needs can create value propositions that are tailored to each customer.

- **Overcome Objections:** Customers often have objections to buying a product or service. By understanding customer needs, salespeople can anticipate these objections and prepare effective responses.

- **Close the Sale:** When salespeople understand customer needs, they can close the sale by showing the customer how their product or service meets those needs.

Different Types of Customer Needs

Customers have three main types of needs:

- **Functional Needs:** These are the basic, tangible benefits that customers seek from a product or service. For example, a customer who is looking for a new car may have functional needs such as fuel efficiency, safety features, and cargo space.

- **Emotional Needs:** These are the psychological and social benefits that customers seek from a product or service. For example, a customer who is looking for a new car may have emotional needs such as feeling safe and secure, feeling stylish, or feeling environmentally friendly.

- **Social Needs:** These are the needs for social approval, recognition, or status that customers may seek from a product or service. For example, a customer who is looking for a new car may have social needs such as wanting to impress their friends and family, wanting to fit in with a certain social group, or wanting to project a certain image.

By understanding the different types of customer needs, salespeople can tailor their sales approach to meet those needs and increase their chances of closing a sale.

Identifying and Understanding Customer Needs

Active Listening:

Active listening is a critical skill for salespeople who want to understand customer needs. Active listening involves paying attention to what the customer is saying, both verbally and nonverbally, and asking clarifying questions to ensure understanding.

Questioning Techniques:

Salespeople can use a variety of questioning techniques to uncover customer needs. Open-ended questions, which cannot be answered with a simple yes or no, are particularly effective for this purpose. Closed-ended questions, which can be answered with a simple yes or no, can be used to confirm information or to narrow down the scope of the conversation.

Empathy:

Empathy is the ability to understand and share the feelings of another person. Empathetic salespeople are better able to understand customer needs and build rapport with customers.

Creating Customer Profiles

Benefits of Creating Customer Profiles:

Customer profiles are detailed descriptions of different customer types, based on their demographics, psychographics, and behavioral data. Customer profiles can help salespeople to

- **Personalize Sales Pitches:** Tailor their sales pitch to the specific needs and interests of each customer.

- **Target Marketing Efforts:** Identify and target specific customer segments with marketing campaigns.

- **Improve Customer Service:** Understand and meet the needs of different customer types more effectively.

How to Create Customer Profiles:

To create customer profiles, salespeople can collect data from a variety of sources, such as:

- **Customer Surveys:** Ask customers about their needs, wants, and buying habits.

- **Sales Data:** Analyze sales data to identify trends and patterns.

- **Market Research:** Conduct market research to learn more about the target market.

Once the data has been collected, it can be used to create customer profiles that include the following information:

- **Demographics:** Age, gender, income, education, occupation, etc.

- **Psychographics:** Personality traits, values, interests, and lifestyle.

- **Behavioral Data:** Purchase history, frequency of purchase, and preferred channels.

Using Customer Profiles:

Customer profiles can be used to better understand and target different customer types. For example, a salesperson who is selling a new software product might create customer profiles for the following types of customers:

- **Small business owners:** These customers are likely to be interested in software that is affordable, easy to use, and can help them improve their efficiency.

- **Enterprise customers:** These customers are likely to be interested in software that is scalable, secure, and can integrate with their existing systems.

- **Individual consumers:** These customers are likely to be interested in software that is user-friendly, has a variety of features, and is available at a reasonable price.

By understanding the needs of each of these customer types, the salesperson can tailor their sales pitch and marketing efforts accordingly.

Anticipating and Influencing Customer Needs

How to Anticipate Customer Needs Based on Market Trends and Customer Feedback:

- **Monitor Market Trends:** Pay attention to emerging trends in the industry and the target market. This can help salespeople to identify new customer needs and opportunities.

- **Analyze Customer Feedback:** Collect and analyze customer feedback from surveys, social media, and customer support interactions. This can help salespeople to identify common customer pain points and areas for improvement.

- **Conduct Market Research:** Conduct market research to learn more about the target market and its needs. This can involve surveys, focus groups, and interviews.

Strategies for Influencing Customer Needs and Creating Demand for Your Products or Services:

- **Educate Customers:** Create content and marketing campaigns that educate customers about their needs and how your products or services can meet those needs.

- **Create a Sense of Urgency:** Use marketing techniques to create a sense of urgency and encourage customers to take action. This can involve limited time offers, discounts, or other incentives.

- **Build Relationships with Customers:** Build relationships with customers through personal interactions, social media, and email marketing. This can help to create trust and loyalty, which can make customers more likely to buy from you.

Examples and Case Studies

Example 1:

A clothing retailer noticed that there was a growing trend for sustainable fashion. In response, the retailer began to offer a line of eco-friendly clothing made from recycled materials. This allowed the retailer to meet the needs of customers who were looking for sustainable fashion options.

Example 2:

A software company noticed that many of their customers were struggling to keep up with the latest software updates. In response, the company developed a new software update that was easier to install and use. This allowed the company to meet the needs of customers who were looking for a more user-friendly software experience.

Case Study 1:

Apple is a company that has achieved sales success through understanding customer needs. Apple's products are designed to be user-friendly and aesthetically pleasing, which appeals to customers' emotional needs. The company also uses celebrity endorsements and social media marketing to create a sense of exclusivity and desirability around its products.

Case Study 2:

Starbucks is another company that has achieved sales success through understanding customer needs. Starbucks' stores are designed to be comfortable and inviting, which creates a positive emotional experience for customers. The company also offers a variety of products to appeal to different customer needs, such as coffee, tea, pastries, and sandwiches.

Conclusion

Salespeople who understand and meet customer needs are more likely to achieve sales success. By anticipating customer needs, influencing customer needs, and building relationships with customers, salespeople can create a positive sales experience that leads to increased sales and customer loyalty.

Actionable Tips for Salespeople to Better Understand and Meet Customer Needs:

1) **Listen to customers:** Pay attention to what customers are saying, both verbally and nonverbally.

2) **Ask questions:** Use open-ended questions to uncover customer needs and pain points.

3) **Be empathetic:** Try to understand the customer's perspective and see things from their point of view.

4) **Educate customers:** Create content and marketing campaigns that educate customers about their needs and how your products or services can meet those needs.

5) **Build relationships with customers:** Build relationships with customers through personal interactions, social media, and email marketing.

Chapter 3

Customer Personas and Segmentation

Customer segmentation and creating customer personas are powerful tools that can help salespeople better understand and target their customers. By dividing the target market into smaller, more manageable segments, and by creating detailed profiles of each segment, salespeople can tailor their sales pitch and marketing efforts to meet the specific needs of each group.

Customer Segmentation

What is Customer Segmentation?

Customer segmentation is the process of dividing a target market into smaller, more manageable groups based on shared characteristics. This allows businesses to tailor their marketing and sales efforts to meet the specific needs of each group.

Different Bases for Segmenting Customers

There are a variety of different bases for segmenting customers, including:

- **Demographics:** Age, gender, income, education, occupation, etc.

- **Psychographics:** Personality traits, values, interests, and lifestyle.

- **Behavioral data:** Purchase history, frequency of purchase, and preferred channels.

Benefits of Customer Segmentation for Sales and Marketing

Customer segmentation offers several benefits for sales and marketing, including:

- **Increased Sales:** By tailoring their sales pitch and marketing efforts to each segment, businesses can increase their sales.

- **Improved Customer Satisfaction:** When customers feel like they are being understood and that their needs are being met, they are more likely to be satisfied with their purchase.

- **Reduced Marketing Costs:** By targeting their marketing efforts to specific segments, businesses can reduce their marketing costs.

- **Improved Efficiency:** By focusing their sales and marketing efforts on the most promising segments, businesses can improve their efficiency.

Customer Personas

What are Customer Personas?

Customer personas are detailed profiles of fictional characters that represent different segments of the target market. These personas are based on research and data, and they help businesses to understand the needs, wants, and motivations of their target customers.

Benefits of Customer Personas for Sales and Marketing

Customer personas offer several benefits for sales and marketing, including:

- **Improved Understanding of Customers:** Customer personas help businesses to better understand the needs, wants, and motivations of their target customers.

- **More Effective Marketing:** By understanding their target customers, businesses can create more effective marketing campaigns tailored to their needs.

- **Improved Sales Performance:** Salespeople who understand their target customers are better able to build rapport and close deals.

Creating Customer Personas

To create customer personas, businesses can use a variety of methods, such as:

- **Surveys:** Conduct surveys to collect data about your target market.

- **Interviews:** Interview customers to learn more about their needs, wants, and motivations.

- **Focus Groups:** Conduct focus groups to get feedback from customers on your products or services.

- **Data Analysis:** Analyze your sales and marketing data to identify trends and patterns.

Once the data has been collected, it can be used to create customer personas that include the following information:

- **Demographics:** Age, gender, income, education, occupation, etc.

- **Psychographics:** Personality traits, values, interests, and lifestyle.

- **Behavioral data:** Purchase history, frequency of purchase, and preferred channels.

Customer personas are a valuable tool for sales and marketing. By understanding the needs, wants, and motivations of their target customers, businesses can create more effective marketing campaigns and improve their sales performance.

Creating Customer Personas

What is a Customer Persona?

A customer persona is a detailed profile of a fictional character that represents a specific segment of the target market. Customer personas are based on research and data, and they help businesses understand the needs, wants, and motivations of their target customers.

How to Create Customer Personas Based on Research and Data

To create customer personas, businesses can use a variety of methods, such as:

- **Surveys:** Conduct surveys to collect data about your target market.

- **Interviews:** Interview customers to learn more about their needs, wants, and motivations.

- **Focus Groups:** Conduct focus groups to get feedback from customers on your products or services.

- **Data Analysis:** Analyze your sales and marketing data to identify trends and patterns.

Elements of a Customer Persona

Customer personas typically include the following information:

- **Demographics:** Age, gender, income, education, occupation, etc.

- **Psychographics:** Personality traits, values, interests, and lifestyle.

- **Behavioral data:** Purchase history, frequency of purchase, and preferred channels.

- **Challenges:** The challenges and pain points that the customer persona is facing.

- **Goals:** The goals and aspirations of the customer persona.

Using Customer Personas in Sales

Customer personas can be used in a variety of ways to improve sales performance, including:

- **Tailor Your Sales Pitch:** By understanding the needs, wants, and motivations of each customer persona, salespeople can tailor their sales pitch to meet the specific needs of each group.

- **Identify and Target Potential Customers:** Customer personas can be used to identify and target potential customers who are most likely to be interested in your products or services.

- **Develop More Effective Marketing Campaigns:** By understanding the customer personas of their target market, businesses can create more effective marketing campaigns that are tailored to their specific needs.

- **Improve Customer Service and Support:** Customer personas can be used to improve customer service and support by helping businesses to understand the needs and expectations of their customers.

Example:

A company that sells software for small businesses might create a customer persona for a small business owner named "Sarah." Sarah is a 45-year-old woman who owns a retail store. She is married with two children and has a college degree. Sarah is looking for a software solution that is affordable, easy to use, and can help her to manage her business more efficiently.

By understanding Sarah's needs, wants, and motivations, the company can tailor its sales pitch to meet her specific needs. For example, the salesperson might emphasize the affordability and ease of use of the software, and how it can help Sarah to save time and money.

Customer personas are a valuable tool for sales and marketing. By understanding the needs, wants, and motivations of their target customers, businesses can create more effective marketing campaigns and improve their sales performance.

Case Study: How Acme Corporation Used Customer Personas to Increase Sales

Company: Acme Corporation

Industry: Consumer Electronics

Challenge: Acme Corporation was struggling to increase sales of its new line of smartphones. The company had a large target market, but it was not clear who the ideal customer was. As a result, the company's marketing and sales efforts were not very effective.

Solution: Acme Corporation decided to create customer personas. The company conducted surveys, interviews, and focus groups with its existing customers to learn more about their needs, wants, and motivations.

Results: Based on this research, Acme Corporation created three customer personas:

- **The Early Adopter:** This persona represented tech-savvy consumers who were always looking for the latest and greatest gadgets. They were willing to pay a premium for a product that was innovative and stylish.

- **The Value Seeker:** This persona represented budget-conscious consumers who were looking for a good deal. They were willing to sacrifice some features for a lower price.

- **The Business Professional:** This persona represented consumers who used their smartphones for work. They were looking for a device that was reliable, secure, and had a long battery life.

Once Acme Corporation had created these customer personas, the company was able to tailor its marketing and sales efforts to each group. For example, the company created different marketing campaigns for each persona, and the sales team was trained to use different sales pitches depending on the customer they were talking to.

As a result of these efforts, Acme Corporation was able to increase sales of its new line of smartphones by 15% in one year. The company was also able to improve its customer satisfaction scores, as customers were more likely to be satisfied with a product that met their specific needs.

Conclusion

Acme Corporation's success story demonstrates the power of customer personas. By understanding the needs, wants, and motivations of their target customers, Acme Corporation was able to create a product line that met the needs of the market and increased sales.

Actionable Tips for Salespeople

Salespeople can use customer personas to improve their sales performance in several ways, including

- Tailor your sales pitch to different customer types.

- Identify and target potential customers most likely to be interested in your products or services.

- Develop more effective marketing campaigns that are tailored to the specific needs of your target market.

- Improve customer service and support by understanding the needs and expectations of your customers.

By following these tips, salespeople can use customer personas to increase sales and improve customer satisfaction.

Chapter 4

Building Trust and Rapport

Trust and rapport are essential for salespeople who want to build strong relationships with customers and increase sales. When customers trust and feel a connection with a salesperson, they are more likely to do business with them.

The Nature of Trust and Rapport

What is Trust?

Trust is the belief that someone is honest, reliable, and competent. It is the foundation of any strong relationship, including the relationship between a salesperson and a customer.

What is Rapport?

Rapport is a connection or understanding between two people. It is based on mutual respect, empathy, and common interests.

The Relationship Between Trust and Rapport

Trust and rapport are closely related. Trust is the foundation of rapport, and rapport is the way that trust is expressed. When salespeople build rapport with customers, they are building trust.

How Trust and Rapport Can Help Salespeople Build Stronger Relationships with Customers and Increase Sales

Trust and rapport are essential for salespeople who want to build strong relationships with customers and increase sales. When customers trust and feel a connection with a salesperson, they are more likely to:

- **Do business with the salesperson:** Customers are more likely to buy from salespeople they trust and feel a connection with.

- **Be loyal to the salesperson:** Customers who trust and feel a connection with a salesperson are more likely to return for repeat business.

- **Refer the salesperson to others:** Customers who trust and feel a connection with a salesperson are more likely to refer them to their friends and family.

Building Trust and Rapport with Customers

There are many things that salespeople can do to build trust and rapport with customers, including:

- **Be honest and transparent:** Salespeople should be honest and transparent with customers about their products or services, their prices, and their policies.

- **Listen actively:** Salespeople should listen actively to customers to understand their needs and concerns.

- **Empathize with customers:** Salespeople should try to understand the customer's perspective and empathize with their needs.

- **Be respectful:** Salespeople should be respectful of customers' time and opinions.

- **Find common ground:** Salespeople should try to find common ground with customers to build a connection.

- **Be yourself:** Salespeople should be themselves and not try to be someone they're not.

By following these tips, salespeople can build trust and rapport with customers and increase their sales.

Building Trust with Customers

Strategies for Building Trust with Customers:

- **Be honest and transparent:** Salespeople should be honest and transparent with customers about their products or services, their prices, and their policies. This means avoiding misleading or deceptive sales tactics.

- **Keep your promises:** Salespeople should keep their promises to customers. This includes delivering products or services on time and as promised and following up with customers after the sale to ensure that they are satisfied.

- **Be responsive to customer needs:** Salespeople should be responsive to customer needs. This means being available to answer questions, address concerns, and resolve problems in a timely manner.

- **Go the extra mile:** Salespeople who go the extra mile for their customers are more likely to build trust. This could involve things like providing personalized service, offering discounts or special promotions, or simply being friendly and helpful.

Building Rapport with Customers

Strategies for Building Rapport with Customers:

- **Find common ground:** Salespeople should try to find common ground with customers to build a connection. This could be anything from shared interests or hobbies to similar backgrounds or experiences.

- **Active listening:** Salespeople should listen actively to customers to understand their needs and concerns. This means paying attention to what they are saying, both verbally and nonverbally, and asking clarifying questions to ensure understanding.

- **Empathy:** Salespeople should try to understand the customer's perspective and empathize with their needs. This means putting themselves in the customer's shoes and seeing things from their point of view.

- **Mirroring and matching:** Salespeople can build rapport with customers by mirroring and matching their body language, tone of voice, and speech patterns. This creates a sense of connection and makes the customer feel more comfortable.

By following these tips, salespeople can build trust and rapport with customers, which will lead to increased sales and customer loyalty.

The Importance of First Impressions

How to Make a Positive First Impression on Customers

- **Dress professionally:** First impressions matter, so it is important to dress professionally when meeting with customers. This shows that you respect them and that you are serious about your business.

- **Be on time:** Punctuality shows that you respect the customer's time. Aim to arrive at meetings or appointments a few minutes early.

- **Smile and make eye contact:** A smile and direct eye contact convey warmth and confidence.

- **Introduce yourself properly:** Introduce yourself clearly and confidently, stating your name, company, and title.

- **Be yourself:** Don't try to be someone you're not. Customers can spot a fake from a mile away.

The Impact of First Impressions on Sales

First impressions have a significant impact on sales. A positive first impression can make a customer more likely to trust and do business with you. Conversely, a negative first impression can make it difficult to build trust and rapport and can even lead to lost sales.

Case Study: How John Smith Built Trust and Rapport to Close a Major Deal

John Smith, a salesperson for a software company, was tasked with closing a major deal with a new customer. The customer was a large corporation with a complex set of needs. John knew that he needed to build trust and rapport with the customer in order to close the deal.

John started by doing his research on the customer. He learned about their business, their needs, and their pain points. He also tried to get to know the key decision-makers on the customer's team.

John built trust with the customer by being honest and transparent. He didn't try to sell them anything they didn't need, and he was always upfront about the costs and benefits of his product.

John also built rapport with the customer by finding common ground. He discovered that he and the customer's CEO were both avid golfers. John used this common interest to build a personal connection with the CEO.

As a result of John's efforts, he was able to build trust and rapport with the customer. This led to a successful close of the deal.

Examples and Case Studies

- **Example 1:** A salesperson for a clothing store noticed that a customer was browsing the racks but seemed hesitant to ask for help. The salesperson approached the customer and offered assistance. The customer was grateful for the help and ended up buying several items.

- **Example 2:** A salesperson for a car dealership went the extra mile for a customer by staying late to help them find the perfect car. The customer was so impressed with the salesperson's service that they bought the car on the spot.

Conclusion

Trust and rapport are essential for salespeople who want to build strong relationships with customers and increase sales. By making a positive first impression, being honest and transparent, and finding common ground, salespeople can build trust and rapport with customers and increase their chances of closing deals.

Actionable Tips for Salespeople to Build Trust and Rapport with Customers:

- Be yourself.

- Be honest and transparent.

- Keep your promises.

- Be responsive to customer needs.

- Go the extra mile.

- Find common ground.

- Listen actively.

- Empathize with customers.

- Mirror and match customers.

Chapter 5

Adapting Your Sales Approach to Different Customer Personalities

Every customer is different, and salespeople need to adapt their sales approach to the different customer personalities they encounter. By understanding the different customer personalities, salespeople can increase their sales effectiveness by tailoring their sales pitch and approach to each customer.

Customer Personalities

There are several different customer personalities, but some of the most common include:

- **The Analytical:** Analytical customers are logical, and data driven. They want to know all the facts and figures before making a decision. Salespeople should focus on providing these customers with detailed information and data to support their claims.

- **The Amiable:** Amiable customers are friendly and easy-going. They are more interested in building a relationship with the salesperson than in hearing a sales pitch. Salespeople should focus on getting to know these customers on a personal level and building trust.

- **The Expressive:** Expressive customers are enthusiastic and outgoing. They are more likely to be swayed by emotional appeals. Salespeople should focus on creating a connection with these customers and showing them how the product or service can benefit them personally.

- **The Driver:** Driver customers are ambitious and goal oriented. They are more likely to be interested in the bottom line. Salespeople should focus on showing these customers how the product or service can help them achieve their goals.

Adapting Your Sales Approach to Different Customer Personalities

Salespeople can adapt their sales approach to different customer personalities by:

- **Identifying the customer's personality:** Salespeople can identify the customer's personality by paying attention to their behavior, their communication style, and their body language.

- **Tailoring their sales pitch:** Salespeople should tailor their sales pitch to the customer's personality. For example, they should focus on providing data and facts for analytical customers, and on building a relationship for amiable customers.

- **Building rapport:** Salespeople should build rapport with the customer by finding common ground and showing empathy.

- **Closing the deal:** Salespeople should close the deal by asking for the sale and overcoming any objections.

By adapting their sales approach to different customer personalities, salespeople can increase their sales effectiveness and build strong relationships with their customers.

Identifying Customer Personalities

Salespeople can identify customer personalities based on their behavior, communication style, and buying preferences.

Behavior

- **Analytical customers:** Analytical customers are often reserved and thoughtful. They may take their time planning and may ask a lot of questions.

- **Amiable customers:** Amiable customers are often friendly and outgoing. They may be more interested in building a relationship with the salesperson than in hearing a sales pitch.

- **Expressive customers:** Expressive customers are often enthusiastic and talkative. They may be more likely to be swayed by emotional appeals.

- **Driver customers:** Driver customers are often direct and to the point. They may be more interested in the bottom line than in building a relationship with the salesperson.

Communication style

- **Analytical customers:** Analytical customers often speak in a logical and data-driven way. They may use facts and figures to support their arguments.

- **Amiable customers:** Amiable customers often speak in a friendly and informal way. They may be more interested in talking about their personal life than about business.

- **Expressive customers:** Expressive customers often speak in an enthusiastic and animated way. They may use emotional language to express their feelings.

- **Driver customers:** Driver customers often speak in a direct and assertive way. They may be more interested in getting down to business than in making small talk.

Buying preferences

- **Analytical customers:** Analytical customers are more likely to research a product or service before making a purchase. They may be more interested in products or services that are backed by data and evidence.

- **Amiable customers:** Amiable customers are more likely to be influenced by the salesperson than by the product or service itself. They may be more interested in products or services that are recommended by someone they trust.

- **Expressive customers:** Expressive customers are more likely to be swayed by emotional appeals. They may be more interested in products or services that are exciting or that make them feel good.

- **Driver customers:** Driver customers are more likely to be interested in the bottom line. They may be more interested in products or services that can help them achieve their goals.

Tailoring Your Sales Approach to Different Customer Personalities

Salespeople can tailor their sales approach to different customer personalities by:

- **Analytical customers:** Salespeople should focus on providing analytical customers with data and facts to support their claims. They should also be prepared to answer any questions that the customer may have.

- **Amiable customers:** Salespeople should focus on building a relationship with amiable customers. They should get to know the customer on a personal level and show empathy for their needs.

- **Expressive customers:** Salespeople should focus on creating a connection with expressive customers. They should show them how the product or service can benefit them personally and use emotional language to appeal to their feelings.

- **Driver customers:** Salespeople should focus on showing driver customers how the product or service can help them achieve their goals. They should be direct and to the point and should avoid wasting the customer's time.

By tailoring their sales approach to different customer personalities, salespeople can increase their sales effectiveness and build strong relationships with their customers.

Case Study: How Sarah Increased Her Sales by 20% by Adapting Her Approach to Different Customer Personalities

Sarah is a salesperson for a software company. She has been in sales for five years, and she has a good track record of success. However, she recently realized that she could be even more successful if she tailored her sales approach to the different customer personalities she encountered.

Sarah started by learning about the different customer personalities. She read books, articles, and blog posts on the topic. She also attended a sales training seminar on customer personalities.

Once Sarah had a good understanding of the different customer personalities, she started to adapt her sales approach accordingly. For example, she:

- **With analytical customers:** Sarah focused on providing them with data and facts to support her claims. She also made sure to answer all of their questions thoroughly.

- **With amiable customers:** Sarah focused on building a relationship with them. She got to know them on a personal level and showed empathy for their needs.

- **With expressive customers:** Sarah focused on creating a connection with them. She showed them how the product or service could benefit them personally and used emotional language to appeal to their feelings.

- **With driver customers:** Sarah focused on showing them how the product or service could help them achieve their goals. She was direct and to the point, and she avoided wasting their time.

As a result of adapting her sales approach to different customer personalities, Sarah was able to increase her sales by 20% in one year. She also built stronger relationships with her customers, which led to repeat business and referrals.

Examples and Case Studies

- **Example 1:** A salesperson for a clothing store noticed that a customer was browsing the racks but seemed hesitant to ask for help. The salesperson approached the customer and offered assistance. The customer was grateful for the help and ended up buying several items. (This is an example of adapting to an amiable customer personality.)

- **Example 2:** A salesperson for a car dealership went the extra mile for a customer by staying late to help them find the perfect car. The customer was so impressed with the salesperson's service that they bought the car on the spot. (This is an example of adapting to a driver customer personality.)

Conclusion

By understanding and adapting to different customer personalities, salespeople can increase their sales effectiveness and build stronger relationships with their customers.

Actionable Tips to Adapt Their Sales Approach to Different Customer Personalities:

- Learn about the different customer personalities.

- Identify the customer's personality.

- Tailor your sales pitch to the customer's personality.

- Build rapport with the customer.

- Close the deal.

Chapter 6

Handling Objections and Overcoming Resistance

Salespeople often encounter objections and resistance from customers. This is a normal part of the sales process, and salespeople need to be able to handle objections and overcome resistance to be successful.

Common Sales Objections

Some of the most common sales objections include:

- **Price objections:** Customers may object to the price of a product or service.

- **Quality objections:** Customers may object to the quality of a product or service.

- **Need objections:** Customers may object to the fact that they don't need the product or service.

- **Competition objections:** Customers may object to the fact that they can get a better deal from a competitor.

How to Handle Objections and Overcome Resistance

Salespeople can handle objections and overcome resistance by:

- **Listening actively:** Salespeople should listen actively to the customer's objection. This shows that they are respecting the customer's opinion and that they are interested in understanding their concerns.

- **Empathizing with the customer:** Salespeople should empathize with the customer's concerns. This shows that they understand where the customer is coming from and that they are not just trying to sell them something.

- **Addressing the objection:** Salespeople should address the objection directly and honestly. They should provide the customer with information that will help them to overcome their objection.

- **Turning the objection into an opportunity:** Salespeople can turn objections into opportunities to build trust and rapport with customers. By showing that they are willing to listen to and address the customer's concerns, salespeople can build trust and show the customer that they are on their side.

Examples of How to Handle Objections

- **Price objection:** "I understand that the price of this product is a concern. However, I can assure you that it is worth the investment. This product is made with high-quality materials and construction, and it is backed by our satisfaction guarantee."

- **Quality objection:** "I understand that you are concerned about the quality of this product. However, I can assure you that it is made with the highest quality materials and construction. We also offer a satisfaction guarantee, so you can be sure that you are making a wise investment."

- **Need objection:** "I understand that you don't think you need this product. However, I can show you how it can benefit you in several ways. For example, this product can help you to save time, money, and energy."

- **Competition objection:** "I understand that you can get a similar product from our competitor for a lower price. However, I can assure you that our product is of higher quality and that we offer better customer service. We also offer a satisfaction guarantee, so you can be sure that you are making a wise investment."

By following these tips, salespeople can handle objections and overcome resistance to increase their sales effectiveness and build strong relationships with their customers.

Handling Objections Effectively

Strategies for Handling Objections Effectively:

- **Listen actively:** Salespeople should listen actively to the customer's objection. This shows that they are respecting the customer's opinion and that they are interested in understanding their concerns.

- **Acknowledge the customer's concerns:** Salespeople should acknowledge the customer's concerns. This shows that they understand where the customer is coming from and that they are not just trying to sell them something.

- **Provide value-based responses:** Salespeople should provide value-based responses to objections. This means that they should focus on the benefits of the product or service and how it can help the customer to solve their problem.

- **Turn objections into opportunities:** Salespeople can turn objections into opportunities to build trust and rapport with customers. By showing that they are willing to listen to and address the customer's concerns, salespeople can build trust and show the customer that they are on their side.

Overcoming Resistance

Techniques for Overcoming Resistance:

- **Identify the customer's underlying concerns:** Salespeople should try to identify the customer's underlying concerns. This may require asking the customer questions to get to the root of their objection.

- **Address the customer's concerns directly:** Salespeople should address the customer's concerns directly and honestly. They should provide the customer with information that will help them to overcome their objection.

- **Offer solutions to the customer's concerns:** Salespeople should offer solutions to the customer's concerns. This may involve offering a discount, a free trial, or a money-back guarantee.

- **Build trust and rapport with the customer:** Salespeople can build trust and rapport with the customer by being honest, transparent, and helpful. They should also show the customer that they are on their side and that they are interested in helping them to solve their problem.

Examples of How to Overcome Resistance

- **Customer:** "I'm not sure if I need this product."

- **Salesperson:** "I understand. Let's talk about your specific needs and see if this product is a good fit for you."

- **Customer:** "I'm worried about the price."

- **Salesperson:** "I understand. This product is a bit of an investment, but it is worth it in the long run. It will save you time, money, and energy."

- **Customer:** "I'm not sure if this product is right for me."

- **Salesperson:** "I understand. Let's schedule a demo so you can try it out for yourself. That way, you can see firsthand how it can benefit you."

By following these tips, salespeople can handle objections and overcome resistance in order to increase their sales effectiveness and build strong relationships with their customers.

Case Study: How John Handled Objections and Overcame Resistance to Close a Major Deal

John, a salesperson for a software company, was tasked with closing a major deal with a new customer. The customer was a large corporation with a complex set of needs. John knew that he would need to be able to handle objections and overcome resistance in order to close the deal.

John started by doing his research on the customer. He learned about their business, their needs, and their pain points. He also tried to get to know the key decision-makers on the customer's team.

John anticipated that the customer would have several objections, such as:

- **Price objections:** The customer might object to the price of the software.

- **Quality objections:** The customer might object to the quality of the software.

- **Need objections:** The customer might object to the fact that they didn't need the software.

- **Competition objections:** The customer might object to the fact that they could get a better deal from a competitor.

John prepared his responses to these objections in advance. He also made sure to practice his delivery so that he could be confident and persuasive when he presented his case to the customer.

When John met with the customer, he was prepared to handle any objections that they might have. He listened actively to their concerns and acknowledged their points of view. He then provided value-based responses to their objections and offered solutions to their concerns.

As a result of John's effective objection handling and resistance-overcoming techniques, he was able to close the deal with the customer. This was a major victory for John and his company.

Examples and Case Studies

- **Example 1:** A salesperson for a clothing store noticed that a customer was browsing the racks but seemed hesitant to ask for help. The salesperson approached the customer and offered assistance. The customer was grateful for the help and ended up buying several items. (This is an example of overcoming resistance by building trust and rapport with the customer.)

- **Example 2:** A salesperson for a car dealership went the extra mile for a customer by staying late to help them find the perfect car. The customer was so impressed with the salesperson's service that they bought the car on the spot. (This is an example of overcoming resistance by offering a solution to the customer's concern.)

Conclusion

By handling objections and overcoming resistance effectively, salespeople can increase their sales effectiveness and build strong relationships with their customers.

Actionable Tips to Handle Objections and Overcome Resistance Effectively:

- Listen actively to the customer's objection.

- Acknowledge the customer's concerns.

- Provide value-based responses to objections.

- Turn objections into opportunities to build trust and rapport with customers.

- Identify the customer's underlying concerns.

- Address the customer's concerns directly.

- Offer solutions to the customer's concerns.

- Build trust and rapport with the customer.

Chapter 7

Closing the Sale

Closing the sale is one of the most important steps in the sales process. It is the point at which the salesperson convinces the customer to buy the product or service. Salespeople who are effective at closing the sale will have higher sales conversion rates and will be more successful in their careers.

The Importance of Closing the Sale

Closing the sale is important for several reasons. First, it is the point at which the salesperson actually generates revenue for the company. Second, closing the sale builds trust and rapport with the customer. When a customer makes a purchase, they are essentially putting their trust in the salesperson and the company. Third, closing the sale can lead to repeat business and referrals. Satisfied customers are more likely to return for repeat business and to refer their friends and family to the salesperson.

The Consequences of Not Closing the Sale

many consequences can occur if a salesperson does not close the sale. First, the salesperson will not generate any revenue for the company. Second, the salesperson may lose the customer's trust and rapport. If a customer feels like they have been pressured into buying something they don't want, they are unlikely to do business with the salesperson again. Third, the salesperson may miss out on repeat business and referrals. Satisfied customers are more likely to return for repeat business and to refer their friends and family to the salesperson.

How to Close the Sale Effectively

There are several different techniques that salespeople can use to close the sale. Some of the most common and effective techniques include:

- **The Assumptive Close:** The assumptive close is a technique in which the salesperson assumes that the customer is going to buy the product or service. For example, the salesperson might say, "Great! I'll have this shipped to your address."

- **The Alternative Close:** The alternative close is a technique in which the salesperson gives the customer two choices, both of which involve buying the product or service. For example, the salesperson might say, "Would you like to pay for this in cash or credit?"

- **The Urgency Close:** The urgency close is a technique in which the salesperson creates a sense of urgency to get the customer to buy now. For example, the salesperson might say, "This offer is only good for a limited time."

- **The Trial Close:** The trial close is a technique in which the salesperson asks the customer if they are ready to buy. For example, the salesperson might say, "Are you ready to take the next step?"

Salespeople should choose the closing technique that they believe is most appropriate for the situation and the customer. It is important to be confident and persuasive when closing the sale, but it is also important to be respectful of the customer's needs and concerns.

By following these tips, salespeople can increase their sales conversion rate and close more deals.

Different Closing Techniques

The Assumptive Close:

The assumptive close is a technique in which the salesperson assumes that the customer is going to buy the product or service. For example, the salesperson might say, "Great! I'll have this shipped to your address."

This technique is effective because it creates a sense of momentum and urgency. It also shows the customer that the salesperson is confident in their product or service.

The Alternative Close:

The alternative close is a technique in which the salesperson gives the customer two choices, both of which involve buying the product or service. For example, the salesperson might say, "Would you like to pay for this in cash or credit?"

This technique is effective because it gives the customer the illusion of choice. However, both choices are ultimately designed to lead the customer to buy the product or service.

The Summary Close:

The summary close is a technique in which the salesperson summarizes the benefits of the product or service and then asks the customer to buy. For example, the salesperson might say, "This product will save you time, money, and energy. Are you ready to take the next step?"

This technique is effective because it reminds the customer of the reasons why they should buy the product or service. It also gives the customer a clear call to action.

The Urgency Close:

The urgency close is a technique in which the salesperson creates a sense of urgency to get the customer to buy now. For example, the salesperson might say, "This offer is only good for a limited time."

This technique is effective because it creates a sense of fear of missing out (FOMO). It also shows the customer that the salesperson is motivated to close the deal.

When to Close the Sale

Salespeople should close the sale when they believe that the customer is ready to buy. There are a number of signs that indicate that a customer is ready to close, including:

- **The customer asks about the price.**

- **The customer asks about the terms of the sale.**

- **The customer asks about the delivery date.**

- The customer says that they are interested in buying the product or service.

- The customer makes a positive comment about the product or service.

Salespeople should be careful not to close the sale too early or too late. If they close too early, the customer may not be ready to buy and may feel pressured. If they close too late, the customer may lose interest or find a better deal elsewhere.

Signs that the Customer is Ready to Buy

Some of the signs that indicate that a customer is ready to buy include:

- The customer is engaged and interested in the conversation.

- The customer asks detailed questions about the product or service.

- The customer makes positive comments about the product or service.

- The customer shows a sense of urgency or excitement.

- The customer asks about the next steps in the process.

When salespeople see these signs, they should be prepared to close the sale.

Overcoming Objections at the Close

Even the most skilled salespeople will encounter objections at the close of the sale. This is a normal part of the sales process, and salespeople need to be prepared to handle objections professionally and effectively.

Some common objections that salespeople may encounter at the close of the sale include:

- **Price objections:** The customer may object to the price of the product or service.

- **Quality objections:** The customer may object to the quality of the product or service.

- **Need objections:** The customer may object to the fact that they don't need the product or service.

- **Competition objections:** The customer may object to the fact that they can get a better deal from a competitor.

Salespeople can overcome objections at the close of the sale by using the following techniques:

- **Listen actively to the customer's objection.**

- **Acknowledge the customer's concerns.**

- **Provide value-based responses to objections.**

- **Turn objections into opportunities to build trust and rapport with customers.**

- **Offer solutions to the customer's concerns.**

- **Close the sale using an effective closing technique.**

Case Study: How John Closed a Major Sale Using an Effective Closing Technique

John, a salesperson for a software company, was tasked with closing a major sale with a new customer. The customer was a large corporation with a complex set of needs. John knew that he would need to be able to handle objections to close the deal.

John started by doing his research on the customer. He learned about their business, their needs, and their pain points. He also made an effort to get to know the key decision-makers on the customer's team.

John anticipated that the customer would have many objections, including price objections, quality objections, and need objections. John prepared his responses to these objections in advance. He also made sure to practice his delivery so that he could be confident and persuasive when he presented his case to the customer.

When John met with the customer, he was prepared to handle any objections that they might have. He listened actively to their concerns and acknowledged their points of view. He then provided value-based responses to their objections and offered solutions to their concerns.

As a result of John's effective objection handling and closing techniques, he was able to close the deal with the customer. This was a major victory for John and his company.

Examples and Case Studies

- **Example 1:** A salesperson for a clothing store noticed that a customer was browsing the racks but seemed hesitant to ask for help. The salesperson approached the customer and offered assistance. The customer was grateful for the help and ended up buying several items. (This is an example of overcoming a need objection by providing value-based assistance.)

- **Example 2:** A salesperson for a car dealership went the extra mile for a customer by staying late to help them find the perfect car. The customer was so impressed with the salesperson's service that they bought the car on the spot. (This is an example of overcoming a price objection by offering a solution to the customer's concern.)

Conclusion

By handling objections and closing the sale effectively, salespeople can increase their sales effectiveness and build strong relationships with their customers.

Actionable Tips for Salespeople to Close the Sale Effectively:

- Be confident and persuasive.

- Listen actively to the customer's objections.

- Acknowledge the customer's concerns.

- Provide value-based responses to objections.

- Turn objections into opportunities to build trust and rapport with customers.

- Offer solutions to the customer's concerns.

- Choose the right closing technique for the situation.

Chapter 8

The Sales Funnel

The sales funnel is a visual representation of the customer journey, from initial awareness to the final purchase. It is a crucial tool for businesses to understand customer behavior, identify potential problems, and optimize the sales process.

Explain its importance:

- **Helps businesses understand customer behavior and identify potential problems:** By analyzing the sales funnel, businesses can see where customers are dropping off and identify areas for improvement.

- **Allows businesses to optimize the sales process and increase conversions:** By understanding the customer journey, businesses can develop more effective marketing and sales strategies to attract, engage, and convert potential customers.

- **Provides insights into customer preferences and buying patterns:** The sales funnel provides valuable insights into customer preferences and buying patterns. This information can be used to tailor marketing and sales strategies to better meet customer needs and increase sales.

Stages of the Sales Funnel:

1. Awareness:

In the awareness stage, the goal is to create awareness and generate interest in the product or service. This can be done through marketing activities such as social media, content marketing, and search engine optimization.

2. Consideration:

Once potential customers are aware of the product or service, they move to the consideration stage. Here, the focus is on providing information and building trust to move prospects further down the funnel. This can be done through educational content, customer testimonials, and product demonstrations.

3. Decision:

In the decision stage, customers are evaluating their options and making purchasing decisions. Factors such as price, features, brand reputation, and social proof influence their choices. Sales representatives play a crucial role in providing personalized recommendations, addressing customer objections, and guiding them towards making a purchase.

4. Action:

The final stage of the sales funnel is the action stage, where customers take action and complete the purchase. It is important to make it easy for customers to take action by providing a seamless checkout process, secure payment options, and clear instructions. Excellent customer service and support are also essential to ensure customer satisfaction and encourage repeat business.

By understanding the stages of the sales funnel and their significance, businesses can develop effective strategies to attract, engage, and convert potential customers into paying customers.

Understanding the Sales Funnel Stages

1. Awareness:

Importance of creating awareness:

- **Introducing the product or service to potential customers:** The first step in the sales funnel is to create awareness and introduce your product or service to potential customers. This can be done through various marketing activities.

- **Generating interest and capturing attention:** Once potential customers are aware of your product or service, you need to generate interest and capture their attention. This can be done by creating compelling marketing messages and content that resonates with your target audience.

Marketing strategies to reach potential customers:

- **Social media marketing:** Social media platforms are a great way to reach and engage with potential customers. You can use social media to share information about your product or service, run contests and giveaways, and interact with customers.

- **Content marketing:** Creating and distributing valuable, relevant, and consistent content is a great way to attract and engage potential customers. This can include blog posts, articles, infographics, videos, and more.

- **Search engine optimization (SEO):** Optimizing your website and content for search engines can help you attract organic traffic from potential customers who are searching for products or services like yours.

- **Paid advertising:** Paid advertising can be a quick and effective way to reach a large number of potential customers. You can use paid advertising platforms like Google Ads and Facebook Ads to target specific demographics and interests.

2. Consideration:

Role of providing information and building trust:

- **Educating prospects about the product or service:** Once potential customers are aware of your product or service, you need to educate them about its features, benefits, and how it can solve their problems. This can be done through product descriptions, FAQs, demos, and other educational content.

- **Building credibility and trust through testimonials, reviews, and demonstrations:** Building trust is essential for moving prospects from the consideration stage to the decision stage. You can build trust by providing customer testimonials, reviews, and product demonstrations.

- **Addressing customer pain points and demonstrating how the product or service can solve their problems:** Identifying and addressing customer pain points is crucial for convincing them to purchase your product or service. Show prospects how your product or service can solve their problems and make their lives better.

By understanding the importance of each stage of the sales funnel and implementing effective strategies to move prospects through the funnel, businesses can increase their sales and grow their customer base.

3. Decision:

Factors influencing customers' purchasing decisions:

- **Price:** Price is a major factor that influences customers' purchasing decisions. Customers are more likely to purchase products or services that are priced competitively and offer good value for money.

- **Features and benefits:** Customers are also influenced by the features and benefits of a product or service. They want to know how the product or service can solve their problems and make their lives better.

- **Brand reputation:** Brand reputation is another important factor that influences customers' purchasing decisions. Customers are more likely to purchase products or services from brands that they trust and have a good reputation.

- **Social proof (testimonials, reviews):** Social proof, such as customer testimonials and reviews, can also influence customers' purchasing decisions. Customers are more likely to purchase products or services that have been recommended by others.

Role of sales representatives:

- **Providing personalized recommendations:** Sales representatives can play a crucial role in helping customers make purchasing decisions. They can provide personalized recommendations based on the customer's needs and preferences.

- **Guiding customers towards making a purchase:** Sales representatives can also help guide customers towards making a purchase by answering their questions, addressing their objections, and providing clear calls to action.

- **Addressing customer objections:** Sales representatives should be prepared to address customer objections and provide satisfactory answers. This can help overcome customer resistance and move them closer to making a purchase.

- **Providing clear calls to action:** Sales representatives should also provide clear calls to action, such as "Buy now" or "Sign up today." This makes it easy for customers to take the next step and complete the purchase.

4. Action:

Importance of making it easy for customers to take action:

- **Seamless checkout process:** The checkout process should be seamless and easy for customers to complete. This includes having a variety of payment options, clear instructions, and a secure checkout process.

- **Secure payment options:** Customers need to feel confident that their payment information is secure when they are making a purchase. Businesses should use reputable payment processors and implement strong security measures to protect customer data.

- **Clear instructions:** Customers should be provided with clear instructions on how to complete the purchase. This includes providing information on shipping, returns, and any other relevant details.

Role of excellent customer service and support:

- **Ensuring customer satisfaction:** Excellent customer service and support are essential for ensuring customer satisfaction. This includes responding to customer inquiries promptly, resolving customer issues quickly and efficiently, and providing friendly and helpful service.

- **Encouraging repeat business:** Excellent customer service and support can also encourage repeat business. When customers have a positive experience with a business, they are more likely to return for future purchases.

By understanding the factors that influence customers' purchasing decisions and making it easy for customers to take action, businesses can increase their sales and grow their customer base.

Monitoring and Optimizing the Sales Funnel

Monitoring the sales funnel is crucial for identifying bottlenecks and areas for improvement. By tracking key metrics and analyzing funnel performance, businesses can gain insights into customer behavior and identify opportunities to optimize the sales process.

Provide tips for tracking key metrics and analyzing funnel performance:

- **Track key metrics:** Some key metrics to track include website traffic, leads generated, conversion rates, and customer lifetime value.

- **Analyze funnel performance:** Analyze funnel performance to identify stages where customers are dropping off. This can help businesses identify areas where they need to improve their sales process.

- **Use sales analytics and CRM systems:** Sales analytics and CRM systems can be used to track key metrics and analyze funnel performance. These tools can provide valuable insights into customer behavior and help businesses optimize their sales process.

Discuss the role of sales analytics and CRM systems in monitoring and optimizing the sales funnel:

Sales analytics and CRM systems play a vital role in monitoring and optimizing the sales funnel. These tools can help businesses:

- **Track key metrics:** Sales analytics and CRM systems can be used to track key metrics such as website traffic, leads generated, conversion rates, and customer lifetime value.

- **Analyze funnel performance:** Sales analytics and CRM systems can be used to analyze funnel performance and identify stages where customers are dropping off.

- **Identify opportunities for improvement:** Sales analytics and CRM systems can help businesses identify opportunities to improve their sales process by providing insights into customer behavior.

Improving Conversion Rates at Each Stage

Awareness:

- **Increase brand visibility:** Increase brand visibility through social media, content marketing, and search engine optimization.

- **Generate leads:** Generate leads through gated content, email marketing, and lead generation forms.

- **Capture prospects' attention:** Capture prospects' attention with compelling headlines, images, and videos.

Consideration:

- **Provide valuable content:** Provide valuable content that educates and informs prospects about your product or service.

- **Build trust:** Build trust by providing customer testimonials, reviews, and case studies.

- **Nurture leads:** Nurture leads through email marketing, personalized recommendations, and retargeting campaigns.

Decision:

- **Address customer objections:** Address customer objections by providing satisfactory answers and demonstrating how your product or service can solve their problems.

- **Provide personalized recommendations:** Provide personalized recommendations based on the customer's needs and preferences.

- **Create a sense of urgency:** Create a sense of urgency by offering limited-time discounts or promotions.

Action:

- **Optimize the checkout process:** Optimize the checkout process by making it seamless and easy for customers to complete.

- **Offer incentives:** Offer incentives such as free shipping or discounts to encourage customers to complete the purchase.

- **Reduce friction points:** Reduce friction points by eliminating unnecessary steps in the checkout process and providing clear instructions.

By monitoring and optimizing the sales funnel and implementing strategies to improve conversion rates at each stage, businesses can increase their sales and grow their customer base.

Case Studies and Examples

Case Study: Nike

Nike is a leading sportswear company that has successfully implemented sales funnel optimization strategies to increase conversions and grow its customer base. Here are some of the tactics and techniques Nike used:

- **Awareness:** Nike increased brand visibility and generated leads through social media, content marketing, and search engine optimization. The company also partnered with influencers and athletes to promote its products and reach new audiences.

- **Consideration:** Nike provided valuable content to educate and inform prospects about its products. The company also built trust by providing customer testimonials, reviews, and case studies.

- **Decision:** Nike addressed customer objections by providing satisfactory answers and demonstrating how its products could solve their problems. The company also offered personalized recommendations and created a sense of urgency by offering limited-time discounts and promotions.

- **Action:** Nike optimized the checkout process by making it seamless and easy for customers to complete. The company also offered free shipping and other incentives to encourage customers to complete the purchase.

Case Study: Amazon

Amazon is a leading e-commerce company that has successfully implemented sales funnel optimization strategies to increase conversions and grow its customer base. Here are some of the tactics and techniques Amazon used:

- **Awareness:** Amazon increased brand visibility and generated leads through social media, content marketing, and search engine optimization. The company also invested heavily in paid advertising to reach new audiences.

- **Consideration:** Amazon provided valuable content to educate and inform prospects about its products. The company also built trust by providing customer testimonials, reviews, and product demonstrations.

- **Decision:** Amazon addressed customer objections by providing satisfactory answers and demonstrating how its products could solve their problems. The company also offered personalized recommendations and created a sense of urgency by offering limited-time discounts and promotions.

- **Action:** Amazon optimized the checkout process by making it seamless and easy for customers to complete. The company also offered free shipping and other incentives to encourage customers to complete the purchase.

Chapter 9

Upselling and Cross-Selling

Upselling is a sales technique in which a salesperson convinces a customer to purchase a more expensive or premium version of the product or service they are considering.

Cross-selling is a sales technique in which a salesperson convinces a customer to purchase additional products or services that complement the product or service they are considering.

Benefits of Upselling and Cross-Selling for Businesses and Customers:

Benefits for Businesses:

- **Increased sales revenue and profitability:** Upselling and cross-selling can help businesses increase sales revenue and profitability by encouraging customers to spend more money.

- **Improved customer satisfaction:** Upselling and cross-selling can also improve customer satisfaction by providing customers with products and services that they need and want.

- **Increased customer loyalty:** Upselling and cross-selling can help businesses build customer loyalty by providing customers with a positive shopping experience.

Benefits for Customers:

- **Access to a wider range of products and services:** Upselling and cross-selling can help customers access a wider range of products and services that they may not have otherwise considered.

- **Convenience:** Upselling and cross-selling can make it more convenient for customers to purchase products and services that they need and want.

- **Personalized shopping experience:** Upselling and cross-selling can help customers feel like they are getting a personalized shopping experience.

Strategies for Increasing the Average Order Value

Practical Strategies for Upselling and Cross-Selling Effectively:

- **Identify upselling and cross-selling opportunities:** Salespeople can identify upselling and cross-selling opportunities by listening to customers' needs and wants. They can also use data and analytics to identify products and services that are frequently purchased together.

- **Present upsell and cross-sell offers in a persuasive and customer-centric manner:** Salespeople should present upsell and cross-sell offers in a persuasive and customer-centric manner. They should focus on the benefits of the products or services and how they can meet the customer's needs.

- **Use effective sales techniques:** Salespeople can use a variety of effective sales techniques to upsell and cross-sell products or services. These techniques include:

  - **Asking open-ended questions:** Open-ended questions encourage customers to talk about their needs and wants. This information can help salespeople identify upselling and cross-selling opportunities.

  - **Active listening:** Active listening is a sales technique in which salespeople pay attention to what customers are saying and respond in a way that shows they understand. This helps to build trust and rapport with customers and makes them more likely to be receptive to upsell and cross-sell offers.

  - **Building relationships with customers:** Salespeople who build relationships with customers are more likely to be successful at upselling and cross-selling. Customers are more likely to purchase products and services from salespeople they know and trust.

By following these strategies, salespeople can increase the average order value and improve sales performance.

The Role of Product Knowledge

Importance of Product Knowledge in Upselling and Cross-Selling:

Product knowledge is essential for upselling and cross-selling success. Salespeople who have a deep understanding of the products or services they sell are better able to identify upselling and cross-selling opportunities and to present these opportunities to customers in a persuasive and compelling manner.

Tips for Salespeople to Develop a Deep Understanding of the Products or Services They Sell:

- **Study product literature and marketing materials:** Salespeople should study product literature and marketing materials to learn about the features, benefits, and uses of the products or services they sell.

- **Attend product training sessions:** Many companies offer product training sessions for their salespeople. These sessions can help salespeople learn about the latest products and services and how to sell them effectively.

- **Talk to product experts:** Salespeople can also talk to product experts within their company to learn more about the products or services they sell. Product experts can provide salespeople with detailed information about the products' features, benefits, and applications.

- **Use product samples:** Salespeople can also use product samples to learn more about the products they sell. Product samples allow salespeople to experience the products firsthand and to see how they work.

How Product Knowledge Helps Salespeople Identify Suitable Upsell and Cross-Sell Opportunities:

Product knowledge helps salespeople identify suitable upsell and cross-sell opportunities by:

- **Understanding the customer's needs:** Salespeople who have a deep understanding of the products or services they sell are better able to understand the customer's needs. This information can help salespeople identify products or services that the customer may also be interested in.

- **Knowing the product line:** Salespeople who are familiar with the entire product line are better able to identify upsell and cross-sell opportunities. They can recommend products or services that complement the customer's initial purchase or that offer additional benefits.

- **Being aware of customer trends:** Salespeople who are aware of customer trends are better able to identify upsell and cross-sell opportunities. They can recommend products or services that are in high demand or that are popular with other customers.

The Role of Customer Satisfaction

Customer satisfaction is closely linked to upselling and cross-selling success. Customers who are satisfied with their purchase are more likely to be receptive to upsell and cross-sell offers. They are also more likely to be repeat customers, which can lead to increased sales over time.

Strategies for Building Strong Customer Relationships and Ensuring Customer Satisfaction:

- **Provide excellent customer service:** Salespeople should provide excellent customer service by being friendly, helpful, and responsive. They should also be knowledgeable about the products or services they sell and be able to answer customer questions.

- **Go the extra mile:** Salespeople can go the extra mile for customers by providing them with personalized service and by taking the time to understand their needs. This can help to build strong customer relationships and increase customer satisfaction.

- **Follow up with customers:** Salespeople should follow up with customers after their purchase to ensure that they are satisfied. This can be done through a phone call, email, or in-person visit. Following up with customers shows that you care about their satisfaction and that you are willing to help them if they have any problems.

How Customer Satisfaction Can Lead to Increased Willingness to Purchase Upsells and Cross-Sells:

Customer satisfaction can lead to increased willingness to purchase upsells and cross-sells in a number of ways:

- **Trust:** Customers who are satisfied with their purchase are more likely to trust the salesperson and the company. This trust makes them more likely to be receptive to upsell and cross-sell offers.

- **Positive experiences:** Customers who have had positive experiences with a company are more likely to be willing to purchase additional products or services from that company. This is because they know that they can expect to receive good value and excellent customer service.

- **Loyalty:** Customers who are satisfied with their purchase are more likely to become loyal customers. Loyal customers are more likely to be open to upsell and cross-sell offers because they know that they can rely on the company to provide them with quality products and services.

Case Studies and Examples

Case Study: Amazon

Amazon is a master of upselling and cross-selling. The company uses a variety of tactics and techniques to increase the average order value, including:

- **Personalized recommendations:** Amazon uses personalized recommendations to suggest products to customers that they may be interested in. These recommendations are based on the customer's past purchase history and browsing behavior.

- **Free shipping:** Amazon offers free shipping on orders over a certain amount. This encourages customers to add more items to their cart in order to qualify for free shipping.

- **Bundle discounts:** Amazon offers bundle discounts on products that are frequently purchased together. This makes it more affordable for customers to purchase multiple products at once.

- **Upsell offers:** Amazon often displays upsell offers on product pages. These offers typically include a more expensive or premium version of the product.

Case Study: Apple

Apple is another company that has successfully implemented upselling and cross-selling strategies. The company uses a variety of tactics and techniques to increase the average order value, including:

- **Product bundling:** Apple bundles its products together in a variety of ways. For example, the company offers a bundle that includes an iPhone, an iPad, and a MacBook. This makes it more convenient and affordable for customers to purchase multiple Apple products at once.

- **Accessories:** Apple sells a wide range of accessories for its products. These accessories can be used to upsell customers who have already purchased an Apple product. For example, Apple sells cases, chargers, and headphones for its iPhones.

- **AppleCare:** AppleCare is an extended warranty program that Apple offers for its products. AppleCare can be used to upsell customers who are concerned about the longevity of their Apple products.

Chapter 10

Sales Follow-Up and Customer Retention

Benefits of Effective Sales Follow-Up and Customer Retention for Businesses:

- **Increased sales:** Effective sales follow-up and customer retention can lead to increased sales. By following up with customers and ensuring that they are satisfied with their purchase, businesses can increase the likelihood that customers will make repeat purchases.

- **Improved customer satisfaction:** Effective sales follow-up and customer retention can lead to improved customer satisfaction. By staying in touch with customers and addressing their concerns, businesses can show customers that they value their business and that they are committed to providing excellent customer service.

- **Positive word-of-mouth:** Effective sales follow-up and customer retention can lead to positive word-of-mouth. When customers are satisfied with their purchase and the customer service they receive, they are more likely to tell their friends and family about their positive experiences. This can lead to new customers for the business.

The Importance of Sales Follow-Up

Why Sales Follow-Up Is Crucial After a Sales Transaction:

Sales follow-up is crucial after a sales transaction for a number of reasons:

- **Thank the customer for their business:** Sales follow-up is an opportunity to thank the customer for their business and to show them that you appreciate their patronage.

- **Ensure customer satisfaction:** Sales follow-up is an opportunity to ensure that the customer is satisfied with their purchase. You can ask the customer if they have any questions or concerns and you can address any problems that they may have.

- **Identify opportunities for additional sales:** Sales follow-up is an opportunity to identify opportunities for additional sales. You can ask the customer if they are interested in other products or services that your company offers.

- **Build customer relationships:** Sales follow-up is an opportunity to build customer relationships. By staying in touch with customers after a sale, you can build trust and rapport with customers and increase the likelihood that they will do business with you again.

Tips for Following Up with Customers in a Timely and Professional Manner:

- **Follow up quickly:** It is important to follow up with customers quickly after a sales transaction. This shows customers that you are responsive and that you value their business.

- **Be personal:** When you follow up with customers, be personal and address them by name. This shows customers that you are taking the time to get to know them and that you value their relationship with your company.

- **Be professional:** When you follow up with customers, be professional and courteous. This shows customers that you are a reliable and trustworthy business.

- **Be helpful:** When you follow up with customers, be helpful and answer any questions or concerns that they may have. This shows customers that you are committed to providing excellent customer service.

Different Channels That Can Be Used for Sales Follow-Up:

- **Phone:** The phone is a great way to follow up with customers. You can have a personal conversation with the customer and you can answer any questions or concerns that they may have.

- **Email:** Email is another great way to follow up with customers. You can send customers a thank-you note, a product update, or a special offer.

- **Social media:** Social media is a great way to stay in touch with customers and to promote your business. You can post updates about your products or services, share customer testimonials, and run contests and giveaways.

Strategies for Effective Sales Follow-Up

Practical Strategies for Following Up with Customers Effectively:

- **Develop a sales follow-up plan:** Before you start following up with customers, it is important to develop a sales follow-up plan. This plan should include the following:

  - The goals of your sales follow-up

  - The target audience for your sales follow-up

  - The channels that you will use for sales follow-up

  - The frequency of your sales follow-up

- **Gather customer feedback:** Customer feedback is essential for improving your sales follow-up process and for ensuring that you are meeting the needs of your customers. There are a number of ways to gather customer feedback, including:

  - Sending customer satisfaction surveys

  - Conducting customer interviews

  - Monitoring customer feedback on social media

- **Address customer concerns:** When you receive customer feedback, it is important to address customer concerns promptly and effectively. This shows customers that you value their feedback and that you are committed to providing excellent customer service.

- **Use sales follow-up to build stronger customer relationships:** Sales follow-up is an opportunity to build stronger customer relationships. By staying in touch with customers after a sale, you can build trust and rapport with customers and increase the likelihood that they will do business with you again.

How to Use Sales Follow-Up to Build Stronger Customer Relationships and Increase Customer Satisfaction:

- **Personalize your follow-up:** When you follow up with customers, personalize your follow-up and address them by name. This shows customers that you are taking the time to get to know them and that you value their relationship with your company.

- **Be responsive:** When customers contact you with questions or concerns, be responsive and answer their questions or concerns promptly. This shows customers that you are committed to providing excellent customer service.

- **Go the extra mile:** Sometimes, the best way to build stronger customer relationships and increase customer satisfaction is to go the extra mile. This could involve providing customers with a free gift, a discount on their next purchase, or simply taking the time to listen to their feedback.

The Role of Customer Satisfaction

Customer satisfaction is essential for sales success. When customers are satisfied with their purchase and the customer service they receive, they are more likely to do business with you again and to recommend your business to others.

Tips for Measuring and Tracking Customer Satisfaction:

There are a number of ways to measure and track customer satisfaction, including:

- **Customer satisfaction surveys:** Customer satisfaction surveys are a great way to get feedback from customers about their experience with your company. You can send customer satisfaction surveys via email, mail, or online.

- **Customer interviews:** Customer interviews are another great way to get feedback from customers about their experience with your company. Customer interviews can be conducted in person, over the phone, or via video conference.

- **Net Promoter Score (NPS):** The Net Promoter Score (NPS) is a metric that measures customer loyalty. NPS is calculated by subtracting the percentage of customers who are detractors (customers who are unhappy with their experience) from the percentage of customers who are promoters (customers who are happy with their experience).

Link Between Customer Satisfaction and Customer Loyalty:

There is a strong link between customer satisfaction and customer loyalty. When customers are satisfied with their purchase and the customer service they receive, they are more likely to be loyal customers. Loyal customers are more likely to do business with you again and to recommend your business to others.

Strategies for Customer Retention

Practical Strategies for Retaining Customers and Increasing Customer Loyalty:

- **Create a customer-centric culture:** A customer-centric culture is one in which the customer is the focus of everything the company does. This means that all employees, from the CEO to the front-line staff, are focused on providing excellent customer service and meeting the needs of customers.

- **Use customer loyalty programs and other incentives:** Customer loyalty programs and other incentives can be a great way to retain customers and increase customer loyalty. Customer loyalty programs typically offer customers rewards, such as discounts, free products, or exclusive access to new products, for making repeat purchases.

- **Provide excellent customer service:** Excellent customer service is essential for retaining customers and increasing customer loyalty. This means being responsive to customer inquiries, resolving customer problems quickly and efficiently, and going the extra mile to meet the needs of customers.

- **Personalize the customer experience:** Personalizing the customer experience can help to build stronger customer relationships and increase customer loyalty. This can be done by using customer data to tailor marketing messages and product recommendations to individual customers.

- **Keep in touch with customers:** Staying in touch with customers after a sale is important for retaining customers and increasing customer loyalty. This can be done through email marketing, social media, or direct mail.

Techniques for Creating a Customer-Centric Culture Within a Business:

- **Empower employees to make decisions:** Empowering employees to make decisions gives them the ability to resolve customer problems quickly and efficiently. This shows customers that you trust your employees and that you are committed to providing excellent customer service.

- **Create a feedback loop:** Create a feedback loop so that customer feedback can be easily shared with employees. This will help employees to understand the needs of customers and to improve their customer service skills.

- **Recognize and reward employees who provide excellent customer service:** Recognizing and rewarding employees who provide excellent customer service shows employees that you value their work and that you are committed to providing excellent customer service.

- **Make customer service a part of your company culture:** Make customer service a part of your company culture by talking about it regularly, by providing customer service training to employees, and by rewarding employees who provide excellent customer service.

How to Use Customer Loyalty Programs and Other Incentives to Retain Customers:

- **Offer a variety of rewards:** Offer a variety of rewards to customers so that they can choose the rewards that are most valuable to them.

This could include discounts, free products, or exclusive access to new products.

- **Make it easy for customers to earn rewards:** Make it easy for customers to earn rewards by offering a variety of ways to earn points. This could include making purchases, referring new customers, or signing up for email marketing.

- **Promote your customer loyalty program:** Promote your customer loyalty program to customers so that they are aware of the benefits of joining. This can be done through email marketing, social media, or in-store signage.

- **Personalize your customer loyalty program:** Personalize your customer loyalty program by offering rewards that are tailored to the individual needs of customers. This can be done by using customer data to track customer preferences and to offer rewards that are relevant to those preferences.

Case Studies and Examples

Case Study: Amazon

Amazon is a master of customer retention. The company has a number of strategies in place to retain customers and increase customer loyalty, including:

- **Customer-centric culture:** Amazon has a customer-centric culture that is focused on providing excellent customer service and meeting the needs of customers.

- **Customer loyalty program:** Amazon Prime is a customer loyalty program that offers members a variety of benefits, including free shipping, exclusive access to new products, and discounts on select items.

- **Excellent customer service:** Amazon provides excellent customer service by being responsive to customer inquiries, resolving customer problems quickly and efficiently, and going the extra mile to meet the needs of customers.

- **Personalized customer experience:** Amazon personalizes the customer experience by using customer data to tailor marketing messages and product recommendations to individual customers.

Case Study: Starbucks

Starbucks is another company that has successfully implemented customer retention strategies. The company has a number of strategies in place to retain customers and increase customer loyalty, including:

- **Customer loyalty program:** Starbucks Rewards is a customer loyalty program that offers members a variety of benefits, including free drinks, discounts on food and merchandise, and exclusive access to new products.

- **Excellent customer service:** Starbucks provides excellent customer service by being friendly and helpful, and by going the extra mile to meet the needs of customers.

- **Personalized customer experience:** Starbucks personalizes the customer experience by remembering customer preferences and by offering personalized recommendations.

Chapter 11

Building Long-Term Relationships with Customers

Building long-term relationships with customers is essential for sales success. Customers who feel valued and appreciated are more likely to do business with a company again and again. They are also more likely to refer their friends and family to the company, which can lead to increased sales and revenue.

The Benefits of Building Long-Term Customer Relationships

There are some benefits to building long-term relationships with customers, including

- **Increased sales and revenue:** Customers who have a long-term relationship with a company are more likely to make repeat purchases. They are also more likely to spend more money with the company over time.

- **Improved customer loyalty:** Customers who feel valued and appreciated are more likely to be loyal to a company. They are less likely to switch to a competitor, even if the competitor offers a lower price.

- **Positive word-of-mouth and referrals:** Customers who have a positive experience with a company are more likely to tell their friends and family about it. This can lead to increased sales and revenue through word-of-mouth and referrals.

- **Reduced customer churn:** Customers who have a long-term relationship with a company are less likely to churn or stop doing business with the company. This can save the company money in marketing and sales costs.

How to Build Long-Term Relationships with Customers

Salespeople can build long-term relationships with customers by:

- **Providing excellent customer service:** Customers want to feel like they are valued and appreciated. Salespeople can provide excellent customer service by being responsive to customer inquiries, resolving customer issues quickly and efficiently, and going the extra mile to meet customer needs.

- **Building trust:** Trust is the foundation of any strong relationship. Salespeople can build trust with customers by being honest, transparent, and reliable. They should also be willing to listen to customer feedback and take customer concerns seriously.

- **Personalizing the customer experience:** Customers want to feel like they are more than just a number. Salespeople can personalize the customer experience by getting to know customers on a personal level, remembering their preferences, and tailoring their sales pitch to each customer.

- **Following up with customers:** Salespeople should follow up with customers after the sale to make sure that they are satisfied with their purchase. They should also stay in touch with customers regularly to provide updates on new products and services, and to offer special promotions.

By following these tips, salespeople can build long-term relationships with customers that will lead to increased sales and customer loyalty.

Strategies for Building Long-Term Customer Relationships

Customers want to feel like they are valued and appreciated. Salespeople can provide excellent customer service by:

- **Being responsive to customer inquiries:** Customers expect salespeople to be responsive to their inquiries. Salespeople should respond to emails and phone calls promptly, and they should be available to answer customer questions on time.

- **Resolving customer issues quickly and efficiently:** When customers have an issue, they want it to be resolved quickly and efficiently. Salespeople should be empowered to resolve customer issues on the spot, and they should be willing to go the extra mile to make sure that customers are satisfied.

- **Going the extra mile to meet customer needs:** Customers appreciate it when salespeople go the extra mile to meet their needs. Salespeople can go the extra mile by providing personalized service, offering discounts and special promotions, and following up with customers after the sale.

Building Trust and Rapport with Customers

Trust is the foundation of any strong relationship. Salespeople can build trust with customers by:

- **Being honest and transparent:** Customers want to feel like they can trust salespeople. Salespeople should be honest and transparent with customers about their products and services, their prices, and their policies.

- **Being reliable:** Customers want to know that they can rely on salespeople to deliver on their promises. Salespeople should be reliable and consistent in their communication with customers.

- **Listening to customer feedback:** Customers want to feel like their feedback is valued. Salespeople should listen to customer feedback and take it seriously. They should also be willing to make changes to their products and services based on customer feedback.

Keeping in Touch with Customers After the Sale

Salespeople should stay in touch with customers after the sale to:

- **Make sure that customers are satisfied with their purchase:** Salespeople should follow up with customers after the sale to make sure that they are satisfied with their purchase. They should also be willing to resolve any issues that customers may have.

- **Provide updates on new products and services:** Salespeople should keep customers informed about new products and services that may be of interest to them. They can do this through email newsletters, social media, or personal phone calls.

- **Offer special promotions:** Salespeople can offer special promotions to customers who have made repeat purchases or who have referred new customers to the company. This is a great way to show customers that they are valued.

Personalizing the Customer Experience

Customers want to feel like they are more than just a number. Salespeople can personalize the customer experience by:

- **Getting to know customers on a personal level:** Salespeople should take the time to get to know customers on a personal level. They can do this by asking customers about their interests, their hobbies, and their families.

- **Remembering customer preferences:** Salespeople should remember customer preferences, such as their favorite products, their preferred method of communication, and their birthday. This shows customers that they are valued and that their business is appreciated.

- **Tailoring their sales pitch to each customer:** Salespeople should tailor their sales pitch to each customer. They should consider the customer's needs, their budget, and their personality.

Case Study: How Acme Corporation Built Long-Term Customer Relationships to Achieve Sales Success

Acme Corporation is a leading provider of software solutions for small businesses. The company has been in business for over 20 years, and it has a long history of building strong relationships with its customers.

Acme Corporation's commitment to customer service is one of the key factors that has contributed to its success. The company's sales team is known for being responsive to customer inquiries, resolving customer issues quickly and efficiently, and going the extra mile to meet customer needs.

Acme Corporation also builds trust with its customers by being honest and transparent. The company's sales team is always upfront with customers about the company's products and services, its prices, and its policies.

Acme Corporation stays in touch with its customers after the sale through a variety of channels, including email newsletters, social media, and personal phone calls. The company also offers special promotions to customers who have made repeat purchases or who have referred new customers to the company.

Acme Corporation's commitment to building long-term customer relationships has paid off. The company has a high customer retention rate, and its customers are loyal and enthusiastic. Acme Corporation's sales have grown steadily over the years, and the company is now one of the leading providers of software solutions for small businesses.

Examples and Case Studies

Example 1: Mary, a salesperson for a software company, built a long-term relationship with a customer named John by going the extra mile to help him solve a problem. John was having trouble getting the software to work properly, and Mary spent several hours on the phone with him, helping him to troubleshoot the issue. John was so grateful for Mary's help that he became a loyal customer and referred several of his friends and colleagues to her.

Example 2: Tom, a salesperson for a car dealership, built a long-term relationship with a customer named Susan by taking the time to get to know her and her needs. Susan was looking for a car that was both fuel-efficient and affordable, and Tom was able to find her the perfect car. Tom also stayed in touch with Susan after the sale, sending her birthday cards and holiday greetings. Susan was so impressed with Tom's thoughtfulness that she became a repeat customer and referred several of her friends and family members to him.

Case Study: How Acme Corporation Achieved Sales Success by Building Long-Term Customer Relationships

Acme Corporation is a leading provider of office supplies and equipment. The company has been in business for over 50 years, and it has a long history of building strong relationships with its customers.

Acme Corporation's commitment to customer service is one of the key factors that has contributed to its success. The company's sales team is known for being responsive to customer inquiries, resolving customer issues quickly and efficiently, and going the extra mile to meet customer needs.

Acme Corporation also builds trust with its customers by being honest and transparent. The company's sales team is always upfront with customers about the company's products and services, its prices, and its policies.

Acme Corporation stays in touch with its customers after the sale through a variety of channels, including email newsletters, social media, and personal phone calls. The company also offers special promotions to customers who have made repeat purchases or who have referred new customers to the company.

Acme Corporation's commitment to building long-term customer relationships has paid off. The company has a high customer retention rate, and its customers are loyal and enthusiastic. Acme Corporation's sales have grown steadily over the years, and the company is now one of the leading providers of office supplies and equipment in the world.

Conclusion

Building long-term relationships with customers is essential for sales success. Salespeople who can build strong relationships with their customers will be more successful in closing deals, increasing sales, and generating referrals.

Actionable Tips for Salespeople to Build Long-Term Relationships with Customers:

- Provide excellent customer service.

- Go the extra mile for customers.

- Build trust and rapport with customers.

- Keep in touch with customers after the sale.

- Personalize the customer experience.

Chapter 12

The Art of Negotiation

Negotiation is a critical skill for salespeople. Salespeople who are skilled negotiators are more likely to close deals, increase their sales revenue, and build strong relationships with their customers.

Basic Principles of Negotiation

There are a few basic principles of negotiation that salespeople should be familiar with, including

- **Preparation is key:** Salespeople should prepare for negotiations by gathering information about the other party, their interests, and their goals. They should also be prepared to make concessions and to walk away from the negotiation if necessary.

- **Understand your negotiation style:** Salespeople should understand their own negotiation style and the negotiation style of the other party. This will help them to adapt their approach and to be more effective in the negotiation.

- **Build rapport:** Salespeople should build rapport with the other party before starting the negotiation. This will help to create a positive atmosphere and to make the negotiation more likely to be successful.

- **Focus on interests, not positions:** Salespeople should focus on the interests of the other party, not on their positions. This will help them to find a solution that meets the needs of both parties.

- **Be creative:** Salespeople should be creative in their approach to negotiation. They should be willing to think outside the box and to come up with new solutions to problems.

- **Be ethical:** Salespeople should always negotiate ethically. They should be honest, transparent, and respectful of the other party.

Different Negotiation Styles

There are a few different negotiation styles that salespeople can use, including:

- **Competitive negotiation:** Competitive negotiation is a win-lose negotiation style in which the goal is to get the best possible deal for yourself, even at the expense of the other party.

- **Collaborative negotiation:** Collaborative negotiation is a win-win negotiation style in which the goal is to find a solution that meets the needs of both parties.

- **Win-win negotiation:** Win-win negotiation is a negotiation style in which both parties are satisfied with the outcome of the negotiation.

The best negotiation style to use will depend on the situation and the other party. Salespeople should be flexible and willing to adapt their style to the needs of the negotiation.

The Importance of Understanding Your Own Negotiation Style and the Negotiation Style of the Other Party

salespeople need to understand their own negotiation style and the negotiation style of the other party. This will help them to adapt their approach and to be more effective in the negotiation.

Salespeople can learn about their own negotiation style by taking a negotiation style assessment or by reflecting on their past experiences. They can learn about the negotiation style of the other party by observing their behavior and by asking questions.

Once salespeople understand their own negotiation style and the negotiation style of the other party, they can develop a strategy for the negotiation. This strategy should be based on the principles of negotiation and should be tailored to the specific situation.

Preparing for a Negotiation

Salespeople can prepare for a negotiation by following these steps:

- **Research the other party:** Salespeople should research the other party to learn as much as they can about their interests, their goals, and their negotiation style. They can do this by talking to people who have negotiated with the other party in the past, by reading about the other party's company, and by observing the other party's behavior.

- **Identify your goals and objectives:** Salespeople should identify their goals and objectives for the negotiation before they start. This will help them to stay focused and to avoid getting sidetracked. Salespeople should also be realistic about their goals and objectives.

- **Develop a negotiation strategy:** Salespeople should develop a negotiation strategy before they start. This strategy should be based on the principles of negotiation and should be tailored to the specific situation. The strategy should include a plan for how to open the negotiation, how to handle objections, and how to close the deal.

Negotiation Techniques

There are many effective negotiation techniques that salespeople can use, including:

- **Active listening:** Salespeople should listen actively to the other party. This will help them to understand the other party's interests and concerns. Salespeople should also pay attention to the other party's body language and nonverbal cues.

- **Empathy:** Salespeople should try to understand the other party's perspective. This will help them to build rapport and to find a solution that meets the needs of both parties.

- **Persuasion:** Salespeople should use persuasion to convince the other party to see their point of view. Salespeople can use data, logic, and emotion to persuade the other party.

- **Concessions:** Salespeople should be prepared to make concessions in order to reach a deal. However, salespeople should not make concessions too quickly or too easily. They should only make concessions when it is in their best interests to do so.

Examples of Effective Negotiation Techniques

- **Example 1:** A salesperson is negotiating the price of a car with a customer. The salesperson starts by listening to the customer's concerns and understanding their budget. The salesperson then presents their own offer, which is slightly higher than the customer's budget. The salesperson uses data and logic to explain why their offer is fair. The customer objects to the price, but the salesperson can persuade them to accept the offer by offering a concession on the financing terms.

- **Example 2:** A salesperson is negotiating a contract with a supplier. The supplier is asking for a higher price than the salesperson is willing to pay. The salesperson uses empathy to understand the supplier's perspective. The salesperson then offers a counteroffer that is lower than the supplier's asking price, but that is still fair. The supplier accepts the counteroffer, and both parties are satisfied with the deal.

By preparing for negotiations and using effective negotiation techniques, salespeople can increase their chances of closing deals and achieving their sales goals.

Overcoming Objections and Resistance in Negotiation

Salespeople can overcome objections and resistance in negotiation by using the following strategies:

- **Handling objections effectively:** Salespeople should handle objections effectively by listening actively to the other party, acknowledging their concerns, and providing value-based responses. Salespeople should also be prepared to make concessions when necessary.

- **Turning objections into opportunities:** Salespeople can turn objections into opportunities by using them to learn more about the other party's interests and concerns. Salespeople can also use objections to build rapport with the other party and to strengthen their own position.

- **Building rapport with the other party:** Salespeople can build rapport with the other party by being friendly, respectful, and understanding. Salespeople should also try to find common ground with the other party.

Closing the Deal

Salespeople can close the deal and reach a mutually beneficial agreement by using the following techniques:

- **Summarize the agreement:** Salespeople should summarize the agreement to make sure that both parties are on the same page.

- **Get a verbal commitment:** Salespeople should get a verbal commitment from the other party before they leave the negotiation.

- **Follow up in writing:** Salespeople should follow up in writing to confirm the agreement and to thank the other party for their time.

Examples of Effective Negotiation Techniques for Closing the Deal

- **Example 1:** A salesperson is negotiating the price of a car with a customer. The salesperson and the customer have agreed on a price, but the customer is still hesitant to sign the deal. The salesperson summarizes the agreement and gets a verbal commitment from the customer. The salesperson then follows up in writing to confirm the agreement and to thank the customer for their time.

By using effective negotiation techniques, salespeople can overcome objections and resistance, close the deal, and reach a mutually beneficial agreement.

Case Studies of Successful Negotiations in Sales

Case Study 1: John Smith Negotiates Major Contract with New Customer

John Smith, a salesperson for a software company, was tasked with negotiating a major contract with a new customer. The customer was a large corporation with a complex set of needs. John knew that he would need to be a skilled negotiator to close the deal.

John started by doing his research on the customer. He learned about the customer's business, their needs, and their pain points. He also made an effort to get to know the key decision-makers on the customer's team.

John developed a negotiation strategy that was based on the principles of negotiation and tailored to the specific situation. The strategy included a plan for how to open the negotiation, how to handle objections, and how to close the deal.

The negotiation was successful, and John was able to close the deal with the new customer. He was able to achieve the customer's goals and objectives, while also meeting the company's goals and objectives.

Case Study 2: Mary Jones Negotiates Favorable Price for Large Order

Mary Jones, a salesperson for a manufacturing company, was tasked with negotiating a favorable price for a large order. The customer was a major retailer, and they were looking for the best possible price.

Mary knew that she would need to be a skilled negotiator to get the best possible price for the customer. She started by doing her research on the customer. She learned about the customer's business, their needs, and their pain points. She also made an effort to get to know the key decision-makers on the customer's team.

Mary developed a negotiation strategy that was based on the principles of negotiation and tailored to the specific situation. The strategy included a plan for how to open the negotiation, how to handle objections, and how to close the deal.

The negotiation was successful, and Mary was able to negotiate a favorable price for the large order. She was able to meet the customer's goals and objectives, while also meeting the company's goals and objectives.

Case Study 3: Tom Brown Negotiates Win-Win Agreement with Difficult Customer

Tom Brown, a salesperson for a consulting firm, was tasked with negotiating a win-win agreement with a difficult customer. The customer was known for being demanding and unreasonable.

Tom knew that he would need to be a skilled negotiator in order to reach a win-win agreement with the customer. He started by doing his research on the customer. He learned about the customer's business, their needs, and their pain points. He also made an effort to get to know the key decision-makers on the customer's team.

Tom developed a negotiation strategy that was based on the principles of negotiation and tailored to the specific situation. The strategy included a plan for how to open the negotiation, how to handle objections, and how to close the deal.

The negotiation was successful, and Tom was able to negotiate a win-win agreement with the difficult customer. He was able to meet the customer's goals and objectives, while also meeting the company's goals and objectives.

Conclusion

By developing and using effective negotiation skills, salespeople can increase their chances of closing deals, achieving their sales goals, and building strong relationships with their customers.

Actionable Tips for Salespeople to Improve Their Negotiation Skills:

- Prepare for negotiations by doing your research and developing a strategy.

- Be a skilled active listener and build rapport with the other party.

- Focus on the other party's interests and concerns.

- Be creative and willing to think outside the box.

- Be ethical and always negotiate in good faith.

Chapter 13

Sales Techniques for Specific Industries

The sales process can vary significantly from one industry to another. This is because each industry has its own unique challenges and opportunities. Salespeople who are successful in a particular industry are those who understand the unique needs of that industry and who tailor their sales approach accordingly.

The Importance of Tailoring Your Sales Approach to Different Industries

There are several reasons why it is important to tailor your sales approach to different industries. First, each industry has its own unique set of customers. These customers have different needs, wants, and expectations. Salespeople who are successful in a particular industry are those who understand the needs of the customers in that industry.

Second, each industry has its own unique set of competitors. These competitors may be using different sales techniques and strategies. Salespeople who are successful in a particular industry are those who are aware of the competitive landscape and who are able to differentiate themselves from their competitors.

Third, each industry has its own unique set of regulations and compliance requirements. Salespeople who are successful in a particular industry are those who are aware of the regulations and compliance requirements that apply to that industry.

Sales Techniques for Different Industries

The following are some specific sales techniques and strategies that are commonly used in different industries:

- **Technology:** Consultative selling and solution-based selling are two common sales techniques that are used in the technology industry. Consultative selling involves working with customers to understand their needs and then recommending the best solution to meet those needs. Solution-based selling involves focusing on the benefits of a product or service and how it can help customers solve their problems.

- **Healthcare:** Relationship selling, and patient-centric selling are two common sales techniques that are used in the healthcare industry. Relationship selling involves building strong relationships with customers and earning their trust. Patient-centric selling involves focusing on the needs of the patient and providing them with the best possible care.

- **Manufacturing:** Technical selling and value-based selling are two common sales techniques that are used in the manufacturing industry. Technical selling involves having a deep understanding of the technical aspects of a product or service. Value-based selling involves focusing on the value that a product or service can provide to customers.

- **Retail:** Suggestive selling, upselling, and cross-selling are three common sales techniques that are used in the retail industry. Suggestive selling involves suggesting additional products or services to customers that they may be interested in. Upselling involves selling customers a more expensive version of a product or service. Cross-selling involves selling customers complementary products or services that they may need.

- **Financial services:** Needs-based selling and wealth management are two common sales techniques that are used in the financial services industry. Needs-based selling involves working with customers to understand their financial needs and then recommending the best products or services to meet those needs. Wealth management involves helping customers to manage their wealth and achieve their financial goals.

Understanding Industry-Specific Challenges and Opportunities

Technology:

- **Challenges:**

    - Rapid technological advancements

    - Evolving customer needs

    - Intense competition

- **Opportunities:**

    - New product development

    - Market expansion

    - Increased efficiency

Healthcare:

- **Challenges:**

    - Regulatory compliance

    - Increasing healthcare costs

    - Changing patient demographics

- **Opportunities:**

    - New medical technologies

    - Growing demand for healthcare services

    - Increased focus on patient experience

Manufacturing:

- **Challenges:**

    - Global competition

  - Supply chain management

  - Rising costs

- **Opportunities:**

  - New markets

  - Product innovation

  - Increased efficiency

Retail:

- **Challenges:**

  - E-commerce growth

  - Changing consumer preferences

  - Increasing competition

- **Opportunities:**

  - Omnichannel retailing

  - Personalization

  - Data analytics

Financial services:

- **Challenges:**

  - Market volatility

  - Increasing competition

  - Regulatory changes

- **Opportunities:**

  - New financial products and services

  - Growing demand for financial advice

- Increased use of technology

By understanding the unique challenges and opportunities of each industry, salespeople can better tailor their sales approach and increase their chances of success.

Case Studies of Sales Success in Different Industries

Technology:

- **Salesperson:** John Smith

- **Company:** Acme Corporation

- **Industry:** Technology

- **Challenge:** Sell a new software solution to a large tech company

- **Solution:** John Smith took the time to understand the customer's needs and pain points. He then developed a customized sales pitch that focused on how the new software solution could help the customer to solve their problems.

- **Result:** John Smith successfully sold the new software solution to a large tech company.

Healthcare:

- **Salesperson:** Mary Jones

- **Company:** Imperial Healthcare

- **Industry:** Healthcare

- **Challenge:** Help a hospital increase patient satisfaction

- **Solution:** Mary Jones built strong relationships with the hospital staff and listened to their feedback. She then worked with the hospital to implement several changes that improved the patient experience.

- **Result:** Mary Jones helped the hospital to increase patient satisfaction scores.

Manufacturing:

- **Salesperson:** Tom Brown

- **Company:** Siemens

- **Industry:** Manufacturing

- **Challenge:** Develop a new sales strategy that would lead to increased sales

- **Solution:** Tom Brown conducted a thorough analysis of the market and the competition. He then developed a new sales strategy that focused on targeting new markets and selling new products.

- **Result:** Tom Brown's new sales strategy led to a significant increase in sales for Siemens.

Retail:

- **Salesperson:** Jane Doe

- **Company:** Main Street Boutique

- **Industry:** Retail

- **Challenge:** Increase sales in a retail store

- **Solution:** Jane Doe used suggestive selling to increase sales in the retail store. She made recommendations to customers based on their needs and preferences.

- **Result:** Jane Doe's use of suggestive selling led to a significant increase in sales in the retail store.

Financial Services:

- **Salesperson:** John Doe

- **Company:** State Street Global Advisors

- **Industry:** Financial Services

- **Challenge:** Provide personalized financial advice to help clients achieve their financial goals

- **Solution:** John Doe took the time to understand his clients' financial needs and goals. He then developed personalized financial plans that were designed to help his clients achieve their goals.

- **Result:** John Doe's personalized financial advice helped his clients to achieve their financial goals.

Conclusion

These case studies demonstrate how salespeople can achieve success in different industries by tailoring their sales approach to the unique challenges and opportunities of each industry.

Actionable Tips to Tailor Their Sales Approach to Different Industries:

- **Understand the industry:** Salespeople should take the time to understand the unique challenges and opportunities of the industry they are selling to.

- **Research the customer:** Salespeople should research the customer's needs and pain points.

- **Develop a customized sales pitch:** Salespeople should develop a customized sales pitch that focuses on how their product or service can help the customer to solve their problems.

- **Build relationships:** Salespeople should build strong relationships with their customers.

- **Be flexible:** Salespeople should be flexible and willing to adapt their sales approach to the needs of the customer.

Chapter 14

Mastering the Sales Mindset

Your mindset is a powerful tool that can either help you or hinder you in your sales career. A positive and resilient mindset can help you to overcome challenges, achieve your goals, and build strong relationships with your customers. On the other hand, a negative and fixed mindset can limit your potential and hold you back from success.

The Power of Mindset in Sales

There are two main types of mindsets that salespeople can have: a fixed mindset and a growth mindset.

Fixed Mindset

People with a fixed mindset believe that their intelligence and abilities are fixed traits. They believe that they cannot change or improve their abilities. This mindset can be limiting because it prevents people from taking risks and trying new things.

Growth Mindset

People with a growth mindset believe that their intelligence and abilities can be developed and improved through effort and hard work. They believe that they can learn and grow from their mistakes. This mindset is empowering because it allows people to take risks, try new things, and learn from their experiences.

The impact of mindset on sales performance

Salespeople with a growth mindset are more likely to be successful than salespeople with a fixed mindset. This is because salespeople with a growth mindset are more likely to:

- **Be resilient:** They are able to bounce back from setbacks and challenges.

- **Be persistent:** They are willing to put in the effort to achieve their goals.

- **Be open to feedback:** They are willing to learn from their mistakes and improve their performance.

- **Be adaptable:** They are able to adapt to changing circumstances and find new ways to succeed.

Actionable Tips for Salespeople to Develop a Growth Mindset:

- **Challenge your negative thoughts:** When you find yourself thinking negative thoughts, challenge them and try to find a more positive perspective.

- **Focus on your effort, not your outcome:** Instead of focusing on the outcome of your sales calls, focus on the effort that you are putting in.

- **Learn from your mistakes:** Everyone makes mistakes. The important thing is to learn from your mistakes and move on.

- **Be open to feedback:** Feedback is a gift. It is an opportunity to learn and improve.

- **Celebrate your successes:** Take the time to celebrate your successes, no matter how small.

By following these tips, you can develop a growth mindset and improve your sales performance.

Developing a Positive and Resilient Sales Mindset

To develop a positive and resilient sales mindset, you can use the following strategies:

Embrace Challenges

Challenges are a part of life, and sales is no exception. Instead of seeing challenges as obstacles, view them as opportunities to learn and grow.

Embrace challenges and use them as a chance to improve your skills and abilities.

Learn from Mistakes

Everyone makes mistakes. The important thing is to learn from your mistakes and move on. Don't dwell on your mistakes or beat yourself up over them. Instead, use your mistakes as an opportunity to learn and improve.

Stay Motivated in the Face of Setbacks

Setbacks are inevitable in sales. There will be times when you don't meet your goals or when you lose a deal. It's important to stay motivated in the face of setbacks. Don't let setbacks discourage you. Instead, use them as a chance to learn and grow.

Overcoming Negative Self-Talk and Limiting Beliefs

Negative self-talk and limiting beliefs can hold you back from achieving your full potential. To overcome negative self-talk and limiting beliefs, you can use the following techniques:

Challenge Your Negative Thoughts

When you find yourself thinking negative thoughts, challenge them and try to find a more positive perspective. For example, instead of thinking "I'm not good enough," you could think "I'm still learning and I'm getting better every day."

Replace Limiting Beliefs with Empowering Beliefs

Limiting beliefs are beliefs that hold you back from achieving your goals. For example, you might believe that "I'm not good at sales" or "I'll never be successful." To overcome limiting beliefs, replace them with empowering beliefs. For example, you could believe that "I'm capable of anything I set my mind to" or "I'm always learning and growing."

Visualize Success

Visualization is a powerful tool that can help you to achieve your goals. Take some time each day to visualize yourself succeeding in your sales career. See yourself closing deals, meeting your goals, and building strong relationships with your customers.

Affirmations

Affirmations are positive statements that you repeat to yourself on a regular basis. Affirmations can help to change your mindset and improve your self-confidence. Some examples of affirmations that you can use include:

- "I am a successful salesperson."

- "I am confident and capable."

- "I am always learning and growing."

- "I am grateful for my customers."

- "I am achieving my goals."

Building Confidence and Self-Esteem

To build confidence and self-esteem, you can use the following strategies:

Set Realistic Goals

One of the best ways to build confidence is to set realistic goals and achieve them. When you set goals that are too difficult, you are setting yourself up for failure. Instead, set goals that are challenging but achievable. As you achieve your goals, your confidence will grow.

Focus on Your Strengths

Everyone has strengths and weaknesses. Instead of focusing on your weaknesses, focus on your strengths. What are you good at? What do you enjoy doing? When you focus on your strengths, you will feel more confident and capable.

Celebrate Your Successes

Take the time to celebrate your successes, no matter how small. When you celebrate your successes, you are reinforcing your positive self-image and building your confidence.

Learn from Your Mistakes

Everyone makes mistakes. The important thing is to learn from your mistakes and move on. Don't dwell on your mistakes or beat yourself up over them. Instead, use your mistakes as an opportunity to learn and grow.

Surround Yourself with Positive People

The people you surround yourself with have a big impact on your self-esteem. Surround yourself with positive people who believe in you and support you. Avoid people who are negative and critical.

Maintain a Positive Attitude

Even in challenging situations, it is important to maintain a positive attitude. When you have a positive attitude, you are more likely to see opportunities instead of obstacles. You are also more likely to be resilient and bounce back from setbacks.

Tips for Maintaining a Positive Attitude

- Start your day with a positive affirmation.

- Focus on the good things in your life.

- Spend time with positive people.

- Avoid negative news and media.

- Do things that you enjoy.

- Be grateful for what you have.

By following these tips, you can build confidence and self-esteem, and maintain a positive attitude. These are essential qualities for sales success.

Case Studies of Salespeople with a Winning Mindset

Case Study 1: Salesperson Overcomes Major Setback to Become Top Performer

John Smith was a successful salesperson, but he faced a major setback when he was diagnosed with cancer. John was forced to take a leave of absence from work to undergo treatment. During his treatment, John remained positive and focused on his goal of returning to work. After completing his treatment, John returned to work and quickly became a top performer again.

Case Study 2: Salesperson Maintains Positive Attitude Despite Facing Numerous Challenges

Mary Jones was a salesperson who faced numerous challenges in her career. She was often assigned to difficult territories and she had to deal with difficult customers. Despite these challenges, Mary maintained a positive attitude and never gave up. She was always willing to go the extra mile for her customers and she always found a way to close the deal.

Case Study3: Salesperson Uses Growth Mindset to Learn from Mistakes and Achieve Success

Tom Brown was a salesperson who made a lot of mistakes early in his career. However, Tom had a growth mindset and he was always willing to learn from his mistakes. He took the time to analyze his mistakes and he developed strategies to avoid making the same mistakes in the future. As a result of his growth mindset, Tom was able to learn from his mistakes and achieve success in his sales career.

Conclusion

The salespeople in these case studies all had a winning sales mindset. They were positive, resilient, and they had a growth mindset. These qualities helped them to overcome challenges, achieve their goals, and build strong relationships with their customers.

Actionable Tips for Salespeople to Develop a Winning Sales Mindset

- Challenge your negative thoughts and replace them with positive thoughts.

- Focus on your strengths and what you are good at.

- Set realistic goals and celebrate your successes.

- Learn from your mistakes and use them as an opportunity to grow.

- Surround yourself with positive people who believe in you and support you.

- Maintain a positive attitude even in challenging situations.

By following these tips, you can develop a winning sales mindset and increase your chances of success.

Chapter 15

Case Studies and Success Stories

Case Study 1: Against All Odds: Mary Johnson's Sales Triumph

Mary Johnson, a young and ambitious salesperson, faced a daunting challenge when she was assigned to a struggling sales territory. The region had consistently underperformed, and many of her predecessors had failed to turn things around.

Undeterred by the odds, Mary approached the challenge with a positive mindset and a determination to succeed. She conducted thorough market research, analyzed customer data, and developed a tailored sales strategy that focused on building relationships and providing value to customers.

Despite initial setbacks and rejections, Mary remained resilient and persistent. She used her setbacks as learning opportunities and adapted her approach accordingly. Gradually, she began to gain traction, winning over customers with her genuine care and expertise.

Within a year, Mary had transformed the struggling territory into a top-performing region. She exceeded her sales targets by a significant margin and became an inspiration to her colleagues. Her success was attributed to her unwavering belief in herself, her ability to learn from her mistakes, and her commitment to providing exceptional customer service.

Case Study 2: From Failure to Fortune: John Smith's Sales Transformation

John Smith, a seasoned salesperson with years of experience, found himself at a crossroads when his sales performance took a downturn. Despite his best efforts, he struggled to meet his targets and was on the verge of losing his job.

Determined to turn things around, John sought the help of a sales coach who introduced him to the power of mindset and self-belief. Through intensive coaching and self-reflection, John realized that his negative self-talk and limiting beliefs were holding him back.

With a newfound positive mindset, John embraced challenges and setbacks as opportunities for growth. He developed a strong belief in his abilities and focused on providing value to his customers.

Gradually, John's sales performance began to improve. He became more confident, resilient, and persistent in his approach. Within a few months, he had not only met his targets but had also surpassed them, becoming one of the top performers in his company.

Case Study 3: Innovation and Success: Kane Williams' Sales Revolution

Kane Williams, a creative and forward-thinking salesperson, was determined to revolutionize the way sales were done in her industry. She believed that by leveraging technology and data, she could create a more efficient and effective sales process.

Kane spent countless hours researching and experimenting with different sales tools and techniques. She developed a unique sales strategy that combined traditional methods with innovative digital solutions.

Initially, Kane faced resistance from her colleagues and superiors, who were skeptical of her unconventional approach. However, she remained steadfast in her belief and continued to refine her strategy.

Over time, Kane's innovative approach proved to be a resounding success. She consistently exceeded her sales targets, closed major deals, and became a sought-after expert in her field. Her success inspired others to embrace innovation and challenge the status quo, leading to a positive transformation in the entire sales team.

Success Stories from the Field

Success Story 1: Rising Above Adversity: Emily Carter's Triumph

Emily Carter, a promising salesperson, faced a major setback when she was diagnosed with a chronic illness. The diagnosis forced her to take a leave of absence from work and undergo extensive treatment.

Determined to overcome her illness and return to her sales career, Emily remained positive and focused on her recovery. She used her time away from work to reflect on her goals and develop new strategies for success.

With unwavering support from her family and colleagues, Emily eventually returned to work, stronger and more resilient than ever before. She approached her sales role with a renewed sense of purpose and a deep appreciation for the opportunity to do what she loved.

Through hard work, dedication, and a positive mindset, Emily quickly regained her momentum and became a top performer once again. Her story is an inspiration to anyone who has faced adversity and demonstrates the power of perseverance and resilience in achieving success.

Success Story 2: The Art of Creative Problem-Solving: David Miller's Sales Magic

David Miller, a seasoned salesperson known for his creativity and problem-solving skills, encountered a challenging customer who seemed impossible to please. The customer had a unique set of requirements and was extremely demanding.

Undeterred by the challenge, David approached the situation with an open mind and a willingness to think outside the box. He spent time understanding the customer's needs and pain points and then developed a creative solution that exceeded the customer's expectations.

David's innovative approach not only closed the deal but also turned the difficult customer into a loyal advocate. The customer was so impressed with David's creativity and customer-centricity that they referred him to several other potential clients.

David's success story highlights the importance of creative thinking and problem-solving in sales. By approaching challenges with an open mind and a willingness to go the extra mile, salespeople can turn even the most difficult situations into opportunities for success.

Success Story 3: The Power of Empathy: Sarah Jones' Customer-Centric Approach

Sarah Jones, a compassionate and empathetic salesperson, always put her customers' needs first. She believed that understanding and addressing her customers' concerns was the key to building lasting relationships and achieving success.

One day, Sarah encountered a customer who was facing a personal crisis that was affecting their ability to make a purchase decision. Sarah listened attentively to the customer's concerns and offered her support and understanding.

Instead of pushing for a sale, Sarah focused on helping the customer find a solution to their problem. She went above and beyond to research different options and provide the customer with the information they needed to make an informed decision.

The customer was deeply touched by Sarah's empathy and genuine concern. Not only did they eventually make a purchase, but they also became a loyal customer who referred Sarah to their friends and family.

Sarah's success story demonstrates the power of empathy and customer-centricity in sales. By prioritizing the customer's needs and providing them with support and understanding, salespeople can build strong relationships and achieve long-term success.

Lessons Learned from the Case Studies and Success Stories:

- **The Importance of Perseverance:** All the salespeople featured in the case studies and success stories demonstrated remarkable perseverance in the face of challenges and setbacks. They never gave up on their goals, even when the odds were against them.

- **The Power of Positive Thinking:** A positive mindset was a common thread among successful salespeople. They believed in themselves, their abilities, and their ability to overcome any obstacle.

- **The Value of Building Relationships:** The salespeople who achieved the greatest success were those who focused on building strong relationships with their customers. They listened to their customers' needs, provided value, and went the extra mile to help them succeed.

Actionable Tips for Salespeople:

- **Embrace Challenges:** View challenges as opportunities for growth and learning. Embrace them with a positive mindset and a willingness to find solutions.

- **Cultivate a Positive Mindset:** Believe in yourself and your ability to succeed. Surround yourself with positivity, whether it's through affirmations, motivational books, or supportive colleagues.

- **Focus on Building Relationships:** Make building relationships with your customers a top priority. Listen to their needs, understand their pain points, and provide them with value.

- **Go the Extra Mile:** Be willing to go the extra mile to help your customers. This could mean providing them with additional information, connecting them with resources, or simply lending a listening ear.

- **Learn from Your Mistakes:** Everyone makes mistakes. The key is to learn from them and move forward. Don't dwell on your mistakes, but instead use them as opportunities to improve.

- **Celebrate Your Successes:** Take the time to celebrate your successes, big and small. This will help you stay motivated and focused on your goals.

By applying the lessons learned from the case studies and success stories, salespeople can increase their chances of achieving their goals and becoming successful in their careers.

Chapter 16

10 Important Sales Strategies

Mastering sales strategy is crucial for sales success in today's competitive business environment. Effective sales strategies enable businesses to identify and target their ideal customers, understand their needs and wants, and develop compelling value propositions. By implementing well-defined sales strategies, businesses can optimize their sales processes, allocate resources effectively, and improve overall sales performance.

Strategy #1: Build Rapport and Trust

Building rapport and trust with prospects is a fundamental sales strategy that lays the foundation for successful sales interactions. When prospects feel connected to and respected by salespeople, they are more likely to be receptive to sales messages, overcome objections, and ultimately make a purchase.

Techniques for making prospects feel understood and respected:

- **Active listening:** Pay attention to what prospects say, both verbally and nonverbally. Ask open-ended questions to encourage them to share their needs, concerns, and desires.

- **Empathy:** Put yourself in the prospect's shoes and try to understand their perspective. Acknowledge and validate their feelings and concerns.

- **Respect:** Treat prospects with respect and courtesy. Avoid interrupting them, making assumptions, or talking down to them.

- **Personalization:** Tailor your sales pitch to the individual prospect's needs and interests. Show them that you've done your research and that you understand their unique situation.

- **Honesty and transparency:** Be honest and transparent with prospects about your products or services. Avoid making promises you can't keep or exaggerating the benefits of your offerings.

Building trust reduces objections and increases close rates:

When prospects trust salespeople, they are more likely to overcome objections and make a purchase. This is because trust reduces the perceived risk associated with buying. Prospects are more willing to take a chance on a product or service if they believe the salesperson has their best interests at heart.

By building rapport and trust with prospects, salespeople can create a positive sales environment that is conducive to closing deals. Prospects are more likely to be receptive to sales messages, overcome objections, and ultimately make a purchase when they feel connected to and respected by salespeople.

Strategy #2: Ask Strategic Questions

Asking strategic questions is a powerful sales technique that enables salespeople to gather valuable information about prospects' needs, challenges, and pain points. By asking the right questions, salespeople can tailor their sales pitch to address the prospect's specific situation and increase the likelihood of closing a deal.

Questions should gather important information to address needs:

- Questions should be open-ended and encourage prospects to elaborate on their answers.

- Focus on uncovering the prospect's needs, challenges, and pain points.

- Ask questions about the prospect's current situation, desired outcomes, and obstacles they are facing.

Prospects purchase solutions, not features - ask them about problems:

- Instead of focusing on the features and benefits of your products or services, ask prospects about the problems they are facing and the outcomes they desire.

- This approach helps you position your products or services as solutions to the prospect's problems.

Using a CRM to track questions and information:

- Use a customer relationship management (CRM) system to track the questions you ask each prospect and the information you gather.

- This information can be used to personalize your sales pitch and follow up with prospects effectively.

Strategy #3: Prepare for and Address Objections

Objections are a natural part of the sales process. Prospects often have concerns or questions about a product or service before they are ready to make a purchase. By anticipating and addressing objections effectively, salespeople can overcome these hurdles and increase their close rates.

Anticipate probable objections based on your solution:

- Think about the common objections' prospects might have about your products or services.

- Consider objections related to price, features, benefits, competition, and risk.

Role play objections with colleagues to craft responses:

- Practice responding to objections with colleagues or other sales professionals.

- Role-playing helps you develop confident and persuasive responses to common objections.

Address objections confidently and turn them into benefits:

- When a prospect raises an objection, listen attentively and acknowledge their concern.

- Then, provide a confident and well-reasoned response that addresses the objection and turns it into a benefit.

- For example, if a prospect objects to the price of your product, you might respond by highlighting the value and long-term benefits of your offering.

By asking strategic questions, anticipating and addressing objections, and using a CRM to track customer interactions, salespeople can gather valuable information, build rapport, and increase their chances of closing deals.

Strategy #4: Tell Compelling Value Stories

Stories are a powerful sales tool that can capture prospects' attention, create emotional connections, and drive sales. When salespeople tell compelling value stories, they are able to communicate the benefits of their products or services in a memorable and engaging way.

Stories are more memorable than features or stats:

- People are more likely to remember stories than they are to remember facts and figures.

- Stories create a lasting impression and help prospects connect with your products or services on a deeper level.

Stories should highlight real customer successes and impacts:

- Share stories of how your products or services have helped other customers achieve their goals or overcome challenges.

- Real-life customer stories add credibility and authenticity to your sales pitch.

Storytelling engages emotions which boosts buying:

- When prospects connect with your stories on an emotional level, they are more likely to be persuaded to make a purchase.

- Emotions play a significant role in buying decisions.

Strategy #5: Demonstrate Product Knowledge

Prospects are more likely to buy from salespeople who are knowledgeable and confident about their products or services. When salespeople demonstrate deep product knowledge, they build credibility and trust with prospects, which increases the likelihood of closing a deal.

Prospects buy from experts, not novices:

- Prospects want to feel confident that they are making a wise purchase decision.

- Salespeople who can demonstrate their expertise are more likely to instill confidence in prospects.

Know your solution inside and out to answer any questions:

- Be prepared to answer any questions that prospects may have about your products or services.

- The more knowledgeable you are, the more credible and trustworthy you will appear.

Deep knowledge builds credibility and confidence:

- When prospects see that you are knowledgeable and confident about your products or services, they are more likely to believe that you are a credible source of information.

- Credibility and confidence are essential for building trust and closing deals.

By telling compelling value stories and demonstrating product knowledge, salespeople can create a positive impression, build trust, and increase their chances of closing deals.

Strategy #6: Use Trial Closes Strategically

Trial closes are a powerful sales technique that can help salespeople gauge a prospect's interest level and move the sales process forward. By asking a series of carefully crafted questions, salespeople can determine whether the prospect is ready to make a purchase or needs more information.

Trial closes gauge interest level before fully presenting:

- Trial closes allow salespeople to assess the prospect's interest level without pressuring them to decide.

- This information can help salespeople tailor their sales pitch and focus on the most relevant aspects of their products or services.

Vary the types of closes used based on prospect's responses:

- There are different types of trial closes that salespeople can use, depending on the prospect's responses and the stage of the sales process.

- Some common types of trial closes include:

  - Assumptive close: "I'll go ahead and process your order. Is that okay?"

  - Alternative close: "Would you prefer the red or blue model?"

  - Yes/no close: "Are you ready to move forward with this purchase?"

Closes should be questions, not commands or pressure tactics:

- Trial closes should be phrased as questions, not commands or pressure tactics.

- Salespeople should avoid being pushy or aggressive, as this can turn prospects off.

Strategy #7: Ask for Referrals and Introductions

Asking for referrals and introductions is a great way for salespeople to generate new leads and grow their pipeline. When salespeople provide value to their customers, they are more likely to receive referrals and introductions to other potential customers.

Reciprocate value by networking for your prospect:

- Salespeople should reciprocate value by networking for their prospects and introducing them to other professionals who can help them achieve their goals.

- This shows prospects that you are genuinely interested in their success and that you are willing to go the extra mile for them.

People do business with people they know and trust:

- People are more likely to do business with people they know and trust.

- By asking for referrals and introductions, salespeople can tap into their network of satisfied customers and generate leads from people who are already familiar with and trust them.

Referral opportunities keep your pipeline full:

- Asking for referrals and introductions is a proactive way to keep your sales pipeline full of qualified leads.

- By consistently asking for referrals, salespeople can ensure that they have a steady stream of potential customers to reach out to.

By using trial closes strategically and asking for referrals and introductions, salespeople can increase their chances of closing deals and growing their business.

Strategy #8: Follow Up Persistently

Follow-up is a crucial part of the sales process. Most sales are made after multiple follow-ups, so it's important for salespeople to be persistent and consistent in their efforts.

Most sales are made after multiple follow ups:

- Studies have shown that it takes an average of 5-12 follow-ups to close a sale.

- Salespeople who follow up persistently are more likely to close deals than those who do not.

Schedule automated follow ups in your CRM:

- Use a customer relationship management (CRM) system to schedule automated follow-ups.

- This will help you stay organized and ensure that you are following up with prospects in a timely manner.

Follow ups should include value, not just chasing for a sale:

- When you follow up with prospects, make sure you are providing value.

- This could include sending them relevant articles, inviting them to webinars, or offering them a free consultation.

Strategy #9: Provide Educational Content

Providing educational content to prospects is a great way to build trust and establish yourself as an expert in your field. When prospects see that you are genuinely interested in helping them learn and grow, they are more likely to do business with you.

Help prospects without expectation of immediate sale:

- When you provide educational content to prospects, do not do it with the expectation of an immediate sale.

- Focus on providing value and helping them achieve their goals.

Content builds expertise, trust and differentiates you:

- By providing educational content, you are demonstrating your expertise and knowledge in your field.

- This helps you build trust with prospects and differentiate yourself from your competitors.

Leverage content as a lead generation and prospecting tool:

- Educational content can also be used as a lead generation and prospecting tool.

- By creating and sharing valuable content, you can attract new prospects and generate leads for your business.

By following up persistently and providing educational content, salespeople can build relationships with prospects, establish themselves as experts, and increase their chances of closing deals.

Strategy #10: Use Social Proof

Social proof is a powerful psychological phenomenon that can influence people's decisions and behaviors. When people see others doing something, they are more likely to do it themselves. In sales, social proof can be used to build trust and credibility with prospects and increase the likelihood of closing a deal.

Case studies and testimonials validate your claims:

- Case studies and testimonials from satisfied customers are a powerful form of social proof.

- They provide prospects with real-world examples of how your products or services have helped others achieve their goals.

Quantify results whenever possible with dollars or metrics:

- When possible, quantify the results of using your products or services in terms of dollars or metrics.

- This makes the benefits more tangible and easier for prospects to understand.

Social proof lowers risk which aids the decision process:

- Social proof can help to lower the perceived risk of buying your products or services.

- When prospects see that others have had a positive experience with your company, they are more likely to believe that they will have a positive experience as well.

By using social proof effectively, salespeople can build trust and credibility with prospects, reduce their perceived risk, and increase their chances of closing deals.

Here are some additional tips for using social proof in sales:

- **Use social proof throughout the sales process:** Social proof can be used at every stage of the sales process, from the initial contact to the close.

- **Use a variety of social proof:** There are many different types of social proof that you can use, such as case studies, testimonials, customer reviews, and social media posts.

- **Make social proof easy to find:** Make sure that social proof is easy for prospects to find on your website, in your sales materials, and on social media.

- **Use social proof ethically:** Only use social proof that is genuine and authentic. Avoid using fake or misleading testimonials.

By following these tips, salespeople can use social proof effectively to build trust, reduce risk, and increase sales.

Chapter 17

5 Best Salespeople of This World and Their Success Secrets

Qualities and Characteristics of a Great Salesperson:

- **Enthusiasm and passion:** Great salespeople are enthusiastic and passionate about their products or services. They are able to convey this enthusiasm to customers, which makes them more likely to buy.

- **Product knowledge:** Great salespeople have a deep understanding of their products or services. They are able to answer customer questions and provide detailed information about the benefits and features of their offerings.

- **Communication skills:** Great salespeople are excellent communicators. They are able to clearly and concisely explain the benefits of their products or services to customers. They are also able to listen to customers' needs and concerns and tailor their sales pitch accordingly.

- **Problem-solving skills:** Great salespeople are able to identify and solve customer problems. They are able to come up with creative solutions that meet the customer's needs and exceed their expectations.

- **Resilience:** Great salespeople are resilient and persistent. They are able to handle rejection and setbacks and continue to move forward. They are also able to learn from their mistakes and improve their sales skills over time.

Five Best Salespeople of This World and Their Remarkable Achievements

- **Joe Girard:** Joe Girard is widely considered to be the world's greatest salesperson. He sold a record 1,425 cars in a single year.

- **Mary Kay Ash:** Mary Kay Ash is the founder of Mary Kay Cosmetics. She built a multi-billion dollar company from scratch and became one of the most successful women in business.

- **Zig Ziglar:** Zig Ziglar is a renowned motivational speaker and sales trainer. He has helped millions of people improve their sales skills and achieve success.

- **Dale Carnegie:** Dale Carnegie is the author of the bestselling book "How to Win Friends and Influence People." His book has helped countless people improve their communication and interpersonal skills, which are essential for sales success.

- **Brian Tracy:** Brian Tracy is a successful entrepreneur, speaker, and author. He has written over 80 books on sales, leadership, and personal development.

Profile of the 5 Best Salespeople

1. Joe Girard: The World's Greatest Salesman

- **Sales techniques and strategies:** Joe Girard was known for his relentless prospecting and follow-up. He would call on potential customers multiple times and never give up until he made a sale. He was also a master of building relationships with his customers. He would remember their names, their families, and their birthdays.

- **Advice for aspiring salespeople:** Joe Girard's advice for aspiring salespeople is to be persistent, to never give up, and to always put the customer first. He also emphasized the importance of building relationships with customers and providing them with excellent service.

- **Followed steps to success:** Joe Girard followed a simple but effective sales process. He would first identify potential customers, then he would build relationships with them, and finally he would close the sale. He was also a master of follow-up and would always stay in touch with his customers after the sale.

2. Mary Kay Ash: The Founder of Mary Kay Cosmetics

- **Sales techniques and strategies:** Mary Kay Ash was a pioneer in the direct selling industry. She developed a unique sales model that empowered women to start their own businesses and sell Mary Kay products. She also emphasized the importance of building relationships with customers and providing them with excellent service.

- **Advice for aspiring salespeople:** Mary Kay Ash's advice for aspiring salespeople is to be passionate about what you do, to be willing to work hard, and to never give up on your dreams. She also emphasized the importance of building relationships with customers and providing them with excellent service.

- **Followed steps to success:** Mary Kay Ash followed a simple but effective sales process. She would first identify potential customers, then she would build relationships with them, and finally she would close the sale. She was also a master of follow-up and would always stay in touch with her customers after the sale.

2. Mary Kay Ash: The Founder of Mary Kay Cosmetics

Followed steps to success:

- **Identified potential customers:** Mary Kay Ash identified potential customers by looking for women who were interested in earning extra income and who had a passion for helping others.

- **Built relationships with customers:** Mary Kay Ash built relationships with her customers by listening to their needs and concerns and by providing them with excellent service. She also made a point of getting to know her customers on a personal level.

- **Closed the sale:** Mary Kay Ash closed the sale by providing her customers with a clear and compelling reason to buy her products. She also made it easy for customers to purchase her products by offering a variety of payment options and by providing excellent customer service.

3. Zig Ziglar: The Motivational Sales Guru

- **Sales techniques and strategies:** Zig Ziglar was a master of motivation and persuasion. He used his sales skills to help people achieve their goals and improve their lives. He was also a strong advocate for positive thinking and self-belief.

- **Advice for aspiring salespeople:** Zig Ziglar's advice for aspiring salespeople is to be enthusiastic, to be positive, and to believe in yourself. He also emphasized the importance of setting goals, taking action, and never giving up.

- **Followed steps to success:** Zig Ziglar followed a simple but effective sales process. He would first identify potential customers, then he would build relationships with them, and finally he would close the sale. He was also a master of follow-up and would always stay in touch with his customers after the sale.

4. Dale Carnegie: The Author of "How to Win Friends and Influence People"

- **Sales techniques and strategies:** Dale Carnegie's sales techniques and strategies are based on the principles of human relations and interpersonal communication. He emphasized the importance of building relationships with customers, understanding their needs, and providing them with excellent service.

- **Advice for aspiring salespeople:** Dale Carnegie's advice for aspiring salespeople is to be sincere, to be interested in others, and to be a good listener. He also emphasized the importance of being positive, enthusiastic, and helpful.

- **Followed steps to success:** Dale Carnegie followed a simple but effective sales process. He would first identify potential customers, then he would build relationships with them, and finally he would close the sale. He was also a master of follow-up and would always stay in touch with his customers after the sale.

5. Brian Tracy: The Sales Training Expert

- **Sales techniques and strategies:** Brian Tracy is a master of sales training and development. He has developed a number of sales techniques and strategies that have helped millions of people improve their sales skills and achieve success.

- **Advice for aspiring salespeople:** Brian Tracy's advice for aspiring salespeople is to be persistent, to be resilient, and to never give up. He also emphasizes the importance of setting goals, taking action, and learning from your mistakes.

- **Followed steps to success:** Brian Tracy followed a simple but effective sales process. He would first identify potential customers, then he would build relationships with them, and finally he would close the sale. He was also a master of follow-up and would always stay in touch with his customers after the sale.

Common Traits and Success Factors

Common Traits Among the Five Best Salespeople:

- **Enthusiasm and passion:** All five salespeople were enthusiastic and passionate about their products or services. They were able to convey this enthusiasm to customers, which made them more likely to buy.

- **Product knowledge:** All five salespeople had a deep understanding of their products or services. They were able to answer customer questions and provide detailed information about the benefits and features of their offerings.

- **Communication skills:** All five salespeople were excellent communicators. They were able to clearly and concisely explain the benefits of their products or services to customers. They were also able to listen to customers' needs and concerns and tailor their sales pitch accordingly.

- **Problem-solving skills:** All five salespeople were able to identify and solve customer problems. They were able to come up with creative solutions that met the customer's needs and exceeded their expectations.

- **Resilience:** All five salespeople were resilient and persistent. They were able to handle rejection and setbacks and continue to move forward. They were also able to learn from their mistakes and improve their sales skills over time.

Key Success Factors:

- **Building relationships with customers:** All five salespeople emphasized the importance of building relationships with customers. They took the time to get to know their customers on a personal level and to understand their needs and concerns. This helped them to build trust and rapport with customers, which made them more likely to buy.

- **Providing excellent customer service:** All five salespeople were committed to providing excellent customer service. They went above and beyond to meet the needs of their customers and to exceed their expectations. This helped them to build a loyal customer base and to generate repeat business.

- **Continuous learning and personal development:** All five salespeople were committed to continuous learning and personal development. They read books, attended seminars, and listened to podcasts to improve their sales skills and knowledge. They were also always looking for ways to improve their products or services and to better meet the needs of their customers.

Great Advice from the Sales Masters

Joe Girard:

- "The greatest thing you can do for your customers is to make them feel important."

- "It's not the size of the sale that counts, it's the number of sales you make."

- "The secret of success is to do the common things uncommonly well."

Mary Kay Ash:

- "There are two things people want most in life: to be appreciated and to be important."

- "Don't be afraid to fail. It's not the failures that count, it's how you handle them."

- "The best way to succeed is to help others succeed."

Zig Ziglar:

- "You can have everything you want in life if you just help enough other people get what they want."

- "The only thing that stands between you and your goal is the story you keep telling yourself why you can't achieve it."

- "It's not what you get in life that counts, it's what you give."

Dale Carnegie:

- "The only way to influence people is to talk about what they want and show them how to get it."

- "A smile is the universal language of kindness."

- "Don't criticize, condemn, or complain."

Brian Tracy:

- "The key to success is to focus on your strengths and improve your weaknesses."

- "The only limits are the ones you set for yourself."

- "Don't wait for opportunity, create it."

Case Studies and Examples

Case Study: Apple

Apple is one of the most successful companies in the world, and its sales team is a major contributor to its success. Apple salespeople are known for their enthusiasm, product knowledge, and customer service skills. They are also experts at building relationships with customers and creating a positive shopping experience.

One of the key sales techniques that Apple salespeople use is to focus on the customer's needs and wants. They take the time to listen to customers and understand their pain points. Then, they tailor their sales pitch to show how Apple products can solve the customer's problems and make their lives better.

Apple salespeople are also very knowledgeable about Apple products. They are able to answer customer questions and provide detailed information about the benefits and features of each product. This helps customers to make informed purchasing decisions and builds trust between the salesperson and the customer.

In addition to their product knowledge and customer service skills, Apple salespeople are also experts at building relationships with customers. They take the time to get to know customers on a personal level and to understand their needs and wants. This helps them to build trust and rapport with customers, which makes them more likely to buy.

Case Study: Amazon

Amazon is another company that has achieved great success through its sales team. Amazon salespeople are known for their customer-centric approach and their ability to provide a seamless shopping experience. They are also experts at using data and analytics to identify customer trends and improve the customer experience.

One of the key sales techniques that Amazon salespeople use is to focus on the customer's journey. They use data and analytics to track customer behavior and identify areas where the customer experience can be improved. They also use this data to personalize the shopping experience for each customer.

Amazon salespeople are also very knowledgeable about Amazon products and services. They are able to answer customer questions and provide detailed information about the benefits and features of each product or service. This helps customers to make informed purchasing decisions and builds trust between the salesperson and the customer.

In addition to their product knowledge and customer service skills, Amazon salespeople are also experts at using data and analytics to improve the customer experience. They use this data to identify customer trends and to personalize the shopping experience for each customer. This helps to increase sales and build customer loyalty.

Chapter 18

Action Plan and Next Steps

Now that you have read this book, it is time to take action and start improving your sales performance. The best way to do this is to develop an action plan. An action plan will help you to set clear goals, identify your strengths and weaknesses, and create a timeline for your goals.

Developing an Action Plan

To develop an action plan, follow these steps:

1. Set Clear Goals

The first step is to set clear goals for yourself. What do you want to achieve in your sales career? Do you want to increase your sales by a certain percentage? Do you want to close a certain number of deals? Once you know what you want to achieve, you can start to develop a plan to reach your goals.

2. Identify Your Strengths and Weaknesses

Once you have set your goals, it is important to identify your strengths and weaknesses. What are you good at? What areas do you need to improve? Once you know your strengths and weaknesses, you can start to develop a plan to capitalize on your strengths and improve your weaknesses.

3. Create a Timeline for Your Goals

Once you know what you want to achieve and what you need to do to achieve it, it is important to create a timeline for your goals. This will help you to stay on track and motivated. When setting your timeline, be realistic about what you can achieve in a given timeframe.

4. Develop Specific Action Steps

The final step is to develop specific action steps that you will take to achieve your goals. These action steps should be specific, measurable, achievable, relevant, and time bound. For example, instead of saying "I want to increase my sales," you could say "I will increase my sales by 15% by the end of the year by making 10 cold calls per day."

By following these steps, you can develop an action plan that will help you to achieve your sales goals. Remember, the key to success is to take action. So, get started today and start working towards your goals.

Overcoming Obstacles

As a salesperson, you will inevitably face obstacles in your career. These obstacles may include rejection, difficult customers, and challenging times. However, there are strategies that you can use to overcome these obstacles and achieve success.

Dealing with Rejection

Rejection is a common part of sales. Not every customer will be interested in what you have to offer. The key is to not take rejection personally. Instead, learn from each rejection and move on to the next opportunity.

Handling Difficult Customers

Difficult customers can be a challenge, but there are ways to handle them effectively. First, try to understand the customer's perspective. What are their needs and concerns? Once you understand the customer's perspective, you can start to develop a solution that meets their needs.

Staying Motivated During Challenging Times

There will be times when sales are slow, and it can be difficult to stay motivated. However, it is important to remember that these challenging times will eventually pass. In the meantime, there are a number of things you can do to stay motivated, such as setting small goals, celebrating your successes, and getting support from your team.

Continuous Improvement

The sales profession is constantly changing. New trends and techniques are emerging all the time. Salespeople need to stay up to date on the latest trends and techniques to stay ahead of the competition.

Tips for Staying Up to Date on the Latest Sales Trends and Techniques

- **Read industry publications.**

- **Attend industry events.**

- **Network with other salespeople.**

- **Take online courses.**

- **Experiment with new sales techniques.**

Sales is a challenging but rewarding career. By following the advice in this book, you can increase your sales performance and achieve success. Remember, the key to success is to act. So, get started today and start working towards your goals.

Take the next steps to improve your sales performance:

- Develop an action plan.

- Set clear goals.

- Identify your strengths and weaknesses.

- Create a timeline for your goals.

- Develop specific action steps.

- Take action and start working towards your goals.

By following these steps, you can achieve your sales goals and become a successful salesperson.